Nicasio Alvarez de Cienfuegos

Twayne's World Authors Series
Spanish Literature

Janet Pérez, Editor
Texas Tech University

TWAS 804

OBRAS POETICAS

DE

DON NICASIO ALVAREZ
DE CIENFUEGOS.

TOMO I.

DE ORDEN DE S. M.
EN LA IMPRENTA REAL
AÑO DE 1816.

From *Nicasio Alvarez de Cienfuegos: Poesías.* Edición de José Luis Cano (Madrid: Editorial Castalia, 1969).

Nicasio Alvarez de Cienfuegos

By Edward V. Coughlin

University of Cincinnati

Twayne Publishers • Boston
A Division of G. K. Hall & Co.

Nicasio Alvarez de Cienfuegos

Edward V. Coughlin

Copyright 1988 by G. K. Hall & Co.
All rights reserved.
Published by Twayne Publishers
A Division of G. K. Hall & Co.
70 Lincoln Street
Boston, Massachusetts 02111

Copyediting supervised by Barbara Sutton
Book production by Gabrielle B. McDonald
Book design by Barbara Anderson

Typeset in 11 pt. Garamond
by Modern Graphics, Inc., Weymouth, Massachusetts

Printed on permanent/durable acid-free paper
and bound in the United States of America

Library of Congress Cataloging-in-Publication Data

Coughlin, Edward V.
    Nicasio Alvarez de Cienfuegos / by Edward V. Coughlin.
        p.   cm. — (Twayne's world authors series ; TWAS 804. Spanish
    literature)
    Bibliography: p.
    Includes index.
    ISBN 0-8057-8236-2
    1. Alvarez de Cienfuegos, Nicasio, 1764–1809—Criticism and
interpretation.   I. Title.   II. Series: Twayne's world authors
series ; TWAS 804.   III. Series: Twayne's world authors series.
Spanish literature.
PQ6503.A52Z6   1988
861'.4—dc19   88–16481
                                                                    CIP

Contents

About the Author
Preface
Chronology

Chapter One
A Short Life   1

Chapter Two
The Early Poems   17

Chapter Three
The Mature Poems   26

Chapter Four
Plays   63

Chapter Five
Minor Works   107

Chapter Six
Conclusion and Summary   116

Notes and References   121
Selected Bibliography   133
Index   137

About the Author

Edward V. Coughlin received a B.A. from Holy Cross College, an M.A. from Boston College, and a Ph.D. from the University of Michigan. He has also studied at the National University of Mexico and the University of Lisbon. Since 1964 he has taught at the University of Cincinnati, where he has served as departmental chair and is now professor of Romance languages.

While he has a special interest in the peninsular literature of the eighteenth and nineteenth centuries, his publications treat the literature of both Spain and Spanish America. In addition to articles that deal primarily with eighteenth-century literature, he has authored or edited the following books: *Antología de la poesía española del siglo XVIII* (1971), *Bibliografía selecta y crítica de Octavio Paz* (1973), *Habides de Ignacio López de Ayala* (1974), *Homenaje a Octavio Paz* (1976), *Adelardo López de Ayala* (1977), *Tres obras inéditas de Ramón de la Cruz* (1979), *Cambios: La cultura hispánica* (1983), *Poems of Roberto Sosa* (1984), *Felipe Godínez: Las lágrimas de David* (1986), and *Ten Unedited Plays of Ramón de la Cruz* (1987).

Preface

This book presents the life and literary contributions of Nicasio Alvarez de Cienfuegos who, despite his relatively short life, was able to attain a preeminent position among the poets and dramatists of the period of transition between neoclassicism and romanticism. I hope that this study will fill an unfortunate vacuum, for this is the first book dedicated solely to Cienfuegos who was, "after Meléndez, perhaps the most outstanding lyric poet of the eighteenth century."[1]

The first chapter is a sketch of Cienfuegos's life, focusing on those activities and friendships that appear to have had an impact upon Cienfuegos the writer. The second chapter deals with the poems Cienfuegos wrote during the years he spent in Salamanca and which remained unpublished until 1968. The third chapter treats the poems written after Cienfuegos had graduated from the University of Salamanca and published in the editions of 1798 and 1816. In this chapter I have emphasized Cienfuegos as a representative poet of the Enlightenment. Although his poetry is widely known, his drama has been forgotten despite the acclaim it received among his contemporaries. Because of this general critical neglect, I have devoted chapter 4 to a consideration of his drama. The final chapter examines his prose writings. These works, like his drama and poems, reveal a man imbued with the spirit of the Age of Enlightenment.

Quotations from the plays are taken from *Teatro de Don Nicasio Alvarez de Cienfuegos* (Barcelona: Imprenta de Antonio Bergnes, 1836), except for *Pítaco*, for which I have used *Teatro español del siglo XVIII*, edited by Jerry L. Johnson (Barcelona: Bruguera, 1972). In all cases I have indicated act and scene in the text at the end of the quotation. All references to Cienfuegos's poetry are from Jose Luis Cano's edition of his poetry, *Poesías* (Madrid: Castalia, 1969) and are cited in the text by the letter *P* and page numbers. I have not placed all comments on his poetics in one chapter; rather, I have discussed meter, musicality, tone, etc., in different parts of the book.

I hope this study will provide the reader with a clear vision of Nicasio Alvarez de Cienfuegos as a writer and as a humane, sensitive, enlightened man.

Edward V. Coughlin

University of Cincinnati

Chronology

1764	14 December, Nicasio Alvarez de Cienfuegos born in Madrid.
1770	Father dies.
1778–1781	Student in the Saint Isidro School (Reales Estudios de San Isidro), Madrid.
1782	Matriculates at the University of Salamanca. Becomes friend of Meléndez Valdés.
1785	Graduates from the University of Salamanca with a degree in law.
1785–1786	Studies for one year in the School of Canon Law of the University of Salamanca.
1787	Returns to Madrid. Becomes friend of Manuel José Quintana.
1789	Obtains bureaucratic position in government.
1792	9 December, premiere of *Idomeneo*.
1797	Becomes member of the Royal Economic Society (Real Sociedad Económica de Amigos del País) and is named official in the Ministry of State.
1798	28 June, premiere of *Zoraida*.
1798	The Imprenta Real publishes a volume containing poetry and dramas. The government names him to head the *Gaceta de Madrid* and the *Mercurio de España*, both official organs of the government.
1799	28 September, delivers eulogy of Joseph Almarza to the Patriotic Society of Madrid. Elected to the Royal Academy of the Language. 24 October, delivers his innaugural address to the Academy.
1801–1808	Receives promotions in the Secretaría del Estado.
1802	11 November, delivers eulogy of the Marquis de Santa Cruz before the Royal Academy of the Language.
1803	23 April, premiere of *La condesa de Castilla*.

1808   Named knight of the Royal Order of Charles III by King Charles IV. 2 May, uprising of the citizens of Madrid against the troops of Napoleon. Orders the proclamation of Fernando VII as king of Spain to be printed in the *Gaceta*. 4 May, refuses to obey demand by French General Murat that he print a retraction of reports concerning Fernando VII. Resigns position in the ministry and editorship of the *Gaceta*. August, Joseph Bonaparte and the French army leave Madrid after the news of the French loss at the Battle of Bailén. December, Napoleon Bonaparte with powerful military force regains control of Madrid.

1809   25 February, Joseph Bonaparte demands government officials swear loyalty to his government. 29 March, dismissed from office for failure to swear loyalty. June, is exiled. Arrives in Orthez, France, on 27 June. 30 June, dies a victim of a tubercular disease exacerbated by his trip into exile.

Chapter One

A Short Life

Cienfuegos lived and wrote in an epoch of crisis. The reign of Carlos IV and the government of Manuel Godoy created a state of affairs that was unsustainable and ultimately resulted in the invasion by Napoleon's troops and the crowning of Joseph Bonaparte as ruler of Spain in 1808. During this period in which Cienfuegos was most active politically and as a writer, Spain was ruled by three people: Carlos IV, an apparently well-intentioned man, but a dull, ineffectual monarch who spent his days at the hunt; his wife, Queen María Luisa, a sensual woman of strong emotions; and her lover, Manuel Godoy, a charming, sensuous man who had neither the training nor the ability to be a truly competent ruler.[1] In what proved to be a portent of future developments, Maria Luisa rather than the heir to the throne convoked the ministers on the day following the death of Carlos III in 1788. It was evident that she and not Carlos IV was going to direct the new government.[2]

In 1793 the king and queen replaced Aranda as their prime minister with Manuel Godoy, a twenty-five-year-old guards officer who had gained the favor of the royal couple and been named lieutenant general of the army, duke of Alcudia, a grandee, and a member of the Council of State. Carlos and María Luisa had honored him with these positions of high rank in part because they distrusted the Francophiles in the ministries. They hoped that Godoy, an inexperienced but ambitious member of the provincial nobility, would be totally loyal to them because he owed them all his distinctions and power.

The relationship of this unusual triumvirate caused great dismay within Spain. Perhaps in a time of greater tranquillity the royal arrangement might have been satisfactory but, unfortunately, the French Revolution and the rise of Napoleon Bonaparte to power disrupted all of Europe including Spain. The government's antirevolutionary policies initiated in response to the overthrow of the French monarchy in 1789 slowed reforms, while the attempts to deal with Napoleon's subsequent rise to power resulted in catastrophe for Godoy and the Bourbons.

After the French Revolution, the Spanish government made considerable efforts to save the life of Louis XVI but to no avail. Upon the king's death in 1793, Spain allied itself with other European monarchies against the French Republic. Soon, however, the French army retaliated by successfully invading Spain, forcing Godoy to seek peace. With the signing in 1795 of the Treaty of Basel for which Godoy received the title "Prince of Peace," Spain lost the Caribbean island of Santo Domingo. Spain again became an ally of France in 1796 with the signing of the Treaty of San Ildefonso, a pledge of mutual military and naval support against Britain. This unfortunate agreement soon led to a declaration of war against England in October of 1796. At first the Spanish and French naval strength forced the British to abandon the Mediterranean, but soon the British navy under Admiral Nelson was victorious in the European sector as well as in the Caribbean with the capture of Trinidad.

Court intrigues in the years 1797 and 1798 brought about sudden changes in Godoy's fortunes. Confronted with an increasing loss of popularity, Godoy attempted to protect his position by taking a different political stance. Therefore, in November 1797 he gained the appointment of Gaspar Melchor de Jovellanos, one of Spain's finest representatives of the Enlightenment, as the minister of grace and justice despite the fact that Jovellanos had earned the queen's enmity by his austerity and criticism of her and the court. Along with this illustrious intellectual, Godoy also brought the talented Francisco Saavedra into the government with the hope of preserving his position of power. Nevertheless, in March of 1798 Godoy's enemies succeeded in having him dismissed as first secretary of state and chief of the royal bodyguard, an act that brought joy to the streets of Madrid, where there was little love for the "sausage maker", as he was called. Godoy's alliance with Jovellanos, Meléndez Valdés, and other intellectuals was merely a temporary affair, although he had had the reputation of being sympathetic toward the intellectual reformers. Interestingly, this period was one of considerable literary activity for Cienfuegos. In 1798 he published a collection of his poems and plays, *Zoraida* had its first performance, and *La condesa de Castilla* was finished although not staged until 1803. The following year, 1799, he entered *Pítaco* in the literary contest sponsored by the Royal Academy of the Language.

The absence of Godoy from the government was short-lived, for within a month he was exercising as much power as usual, although the ministers Jovellanos and Saavedra bore the responsibility. In August 1798 a mysterious illness, perhaps caused by poison, struck Jovellanos and his chief associate. That same month Jovellanos was relieved of his ministry and ordered to return to his native Asturias (which did not displease him because his character was unsuited to life in the corrupt court). With these sudden turns of events Godoy, although without portfolio, regained his complete authority as the royal favorite.[3] The great turmoil in the government owed, in part, to the minister José Caballero, a reactionary opposed to the progressive ideas of the Enlightenment, who "swept the intellectuals and 'Jansenists' from office and instilled anew a fear of France and progress in the court. Thus a great event like the French Revolution had little resonance in Spanish opinion and the efforts at revolutionary propaganda had little success."[4]

Cienfuegos, who was ideologically close to Jovellanos, must have been deeply touched by the sordid afairs of the court for some time, but even more so when Jovellanos, a man whom he admired as a literary mentor, suffered from the hypocrisy and intrigues of the court.[5] Given the corrupt political situation and Cienfuego's friendship and association with progressive thinkers like Manuel José Quintana, one can justifiably interpret his works, especially his drama, as a commentary on the contemporary state of affairs within Spain and a direct lesson for the royal family on the qualities and attitude required of an enlightened monarch.

Cienfuegos was not alone in his attacks. Raymond Carr reports other intellectuals were also highly critical of Spanish society during this important period of Spanish history.[6] Examples of this criticism survive in Goya's *Caprichos* and in the humanitarian poems of Meléndez Valdés and Cienfuegos. One of the most radical figures was the cleric Marchena, who appealed "to Spain to destroy the Inquisition and imitate the 'sublime' revolution of France."[7] This radical Jacobinism, however, was by no means common. More usual and, therefore, more important was the increasing popularity of the idea that the monarch's power should be limited by a constitution. The standard argument in favor of reducing the powers of a monarch contended that absolute power requires an impossible absolute wisdom. Although recognizing the beneficent use of such power in carrying out reforms, they saw the need to limit it "in the event of its being exercised by an irresponsible favourite like Godoy."[8]

To appreciate fully the writings of Nicasio Alvarez de Cienfuegos,

it is essential to consider the ideas and goals of the Spanish nation
at the turn of the century. It is not surprising that a poet of his
epoch would take an active role in politics and participate in the
ideological struggles. The Age of Enlightenment, probably more
than other epochs, demanded a great deal from its intellectual and
literary class. Cienfuegos, like his friends Meléndez Valdés, Quintana, and Jovellanos, demonstrates the commitment to social, political, and economic reforms that typifies the leaders of the
Enlightenment throughout Europe and the Americas.

The Early Years

Nicasio Alvarez de Cienfuegos was born in Madrid on 14 December 1764 in a house on what is now the Calle de la Colegiata
and which in the eighteenth century was known as the Calle de la
Compañía. Although his father, also named Nicasio, was a native
of Garrovillas, Cáceres, the Alvarez de Cienfuegos family (of the
minor nobility) originated from Asturias.[9] The poet's mother, Manuela Acero, was born in Madrid of a Castilian family. In addition
to Nicasio, the couple had a daughter named Vicenta. When Nicasio's father died in 1770 Doña Manuela had to raise their children
alone. The loss of his father, when Nicasio was still in his fifth
year, undoubtedly had a profound psychological effect upon him.
From that time on his mother, who had limited resources, was to
be his only emotional and financial support. Nicasio's dedication of
his comedy *Las hermanas generosas* (The generous sisters) reveals the
affection he held for his mother, who had to struggle continuously
in order to provide her son with any advantage she could. Cienfuegos's close relationship with his mother could be a partial explanation
for his extremely sensitive and sentimental nature. However, the
spirit of the time and later friendships were undoubtedly greater
factors in the development of his literary personality.

In the dedication of *The Generous Sisters* he idealizes his mother
who, upon being left a widow at age twenty-six, dedicated herself
to making "the most heroic sacrifices for my future happiness. . . .
Alone against the world, haven't I seen you struggle on my behalf
without help, poverty stricken, and forced to suffer the embarrass-
ment and contempt of being poor?"[10] His mother must have been
an extraordinarily kind, generous, and strong woman to elicit his
effusive sentimental dedication—a modern reader might describe it

as maudlin—which lays the foundation for the excessively emotional tone of *The Generous Sisters.*

Doña Manuela clearly succeeded in providing Nicasio with a superior education. He first studied Latin and rhetoric at the Colegio de la Escuelas Pías in Getafe near Madrid. Later he attended the Reales Estudios de San Isidro in the capital where, from 1778 to 1781, he studied Greek, logic, moral philosophy, and mathematics. Proof that he was an excellent student at the Reales Estudios de San Isidro, a secular secondary school the government had opened in the buildings of the Colegio Imperial formerly run by the Jesuits, is the fact that he participated in the *conclusiones* in almost every class in which he was enrolled.[11] Only the most outstanding students were permitted to participate in these academic events, which occurred at the conclusion of the course and were open to the public.

University Studies

During the 1781–82 academic year Cienfuegos studied at the law school of the University of Oñate in the province of Guipuzcoa. For unknown reasons he did not continue his studies there. In 1782, at the age of seventeen, he enrolled in the University of Salamanca as a second-year student of law. Juan Meléndez Valdés, already a recognized poet, was a member of the board that judged Cienfuegos's qualifications for matriculation in Spain's oldest university. Having passed the entrance examination, Cienfuegos decided to study law. In the academic year of 1784–85 he enrolled in the first-year classes of the School of Canon Law. The Plan de Estudios of 1771 suggests that it probably was common for the students of law to spend a year studying canon or civil law according to one's specialization.[12] Cienfuegos graduated with a degree in law on 2 June 1785 after achieving a distinguished academic record. The following academic year, 1785–86, he again enrolled in the School of Canon Law, where he studied the second-year courses. He probably intended to obtain a degree from that faculty, as he enrolled for the third year of canon law, but his name does not appear in the record of the final examination for the 1786–87 academic year.

On 10 November 1785, at the meeting of the governing board *(claustro)* of the university, Cienfuegos was elected a *consiliario* and on 2 December took possession of that office. A dispute arose over the fact that he was twenty-one while the university statutes required that a person holding the position of *consiliario* be twenty-four. Cienfuegos was not the first to break the rule, and eventually the case was decided in his favor. He continued to serve on the university's governing board at least until December of 1786. He apparently was absent from Salamanca during part of that school year, and in April 1787 Manuel Urquijo was nominated to replace him as a *consiliario*.

The five years that Cienfuegos spent in Salamanca were pleasant ones. Close friendships with various men of letters had a lasting impact upon the life of the poet and dramatist. His affectionate, sentimental vision of the university city appears in an autobiographical poem entitled "El recuerdo de mi adolescencia" (The memory of my youth) which was addressed to Batilo, the poetic name of his beloved teacher and friend Juan Meléndez Valdés. The final verses of the poem recall his pleasant university days. The intense emotion of these verses reveals the profound impact of the Salamanca experience upon Cienfuegos.

The intellectual environment created by his professorial and literary friends formed the young student both intellectually and poetically. The years at the University of Salamanca were crucial ones for Cienfuegos, owing in great part to his close relationship with the distinguished poet and professor Meléndez Valdés, who became the youth's spiritual guide. He awakened an interest in poetry in Cienfuegos, who began to write verse after his arrival in Salamanca. These early poems reflect in style and content the influence of Meléndez Valdés, whose friendship and guidance probably changed the young student's life. A crucial experience for Cienfuegos was the opportunity to participate with kindred spirits who gathered in Meléndez's home to discuss literature and the ideas of the Enlightenment. Among the poets and scholars who belonged to the circle of Meléndez's friends were José Iglesias de la Casa, Fray Diego González, Professor Candamo, and Father Fernández de Rojas. The sensitive young man must have been overjoyed to be able to associate with these distinguished individuals and to take part in their discussions.

Melendez's friends welcomed both the old and the new.[13] Dedicated to the traditional study of the humanities, they appreciated the classics and enthusiastically welcomed the ideas of contemporary Europeans. They read Homer, Vergil, Anacreon, and Horace as well as Locke, Condillac, Montesquieu, Rousseau, Saint-Lambert, and

Young.[14] Interest in one group did not impede an appreciation for the other.

Cienfuegos and his friends were able to obtain a wide selection of books by French authors, some of whom were prohibited by the censors. The bookseller Alegría, whose bookstore was near the university, secretly imported books from France for those who desired to keep abreast of the European political and literary scenes. It is clear that, despite a prohibition of his works "to all classes of readers in the Spanish world in 1764,"[15] Rousseau had a great influence upon Spanish writers of the eighteenth century, including Cienfuegos. Cienfuegos must have absorbed many ideas of the Enlightenment during his years in Salamanca. Such themes as equality, universal brotherhood, and love of virtue which are so prominent in his poetry and theater must have become part of his emotional and intellectual personality as a result of his experiences in Salamanca.

Return to Madrid

In 1787 Cienfuegos left Salamanca to return to Madrid to live with his mother. Besides a law degree, he had also acquired a broad background in the humanities and had written a few poems. At this point, he planned, in collaboration with his friend Juan de Peñalver, an edition of the poetry of the Renaissance poet Fernando de Herrera.[16] There is no evidence that Cienfuegos and Peñalver ever finished their project. Cienfuegos apparently hoped for a literary career in Madrid, but he soon realized that such a vocation would not provide sufficient income to support himself and his mother. Thus he turned to his legal training, and probably with the aid of Meléndez Valdés and the distinguished polygraph, jurist, and statesman Gaspar Melchor de Jovellanos he acquired a government position as a lawyer of the Reales Consejos on 3 November 1789.[17]

Not long after returning to Madrid from the University of Salamanca, Cienfuegos developed a close and important friendship with Manuel José Quintana, eight years his junior, who also studied under Meléndez Valdés in Salamanca. There is considerable testimony of Cienfuegos's close friendship with Quintana. For example, in 1802 Quintana published a poem to Cienfuegos, "A D. Nicasio Cienfuegos convidándole a gozar del campo" (To Nicasio Cienfuegos inviting him to enjoy the country). The opening verses reveal the poet's admiration and affection for Cienfuegos: "You, whom heaven

looked upon / with kind eyes from birth; you, in whose breast /
heaven imprinted virtue, and with a generous hand / gave the divine
gift of painting it."[18] Quintana's affection for his friend is also
evident in the prologue he wrote for the 1813 edition of his poetry.
Here Quintana also confesses to Cienfuegos's influence upon his
writings.

Cienfuegos shared with his friend a similar liberal view of politics
and society. In fact, their intellectual circle has been considered to
be the most radical wing of the Spanish Enlightenment. The conservative Marcelino Menéndez Pelayo believed Quintana to be a true
revolutionary, prepared to make drastic changes in Spanish society.[19]
The writer and politician Antonio Alcalá Galiano, who was then a
very young man, attended the gatherings of Quintana's friends at
his home in Madrid where they discussed politics and literature.
He reports that among the poets and intellectuals who met at Quintana's home were Juan Bautista Arriaza, Manuel María de Arjona
de Cubas, Eugenio de Tapia, Juan Nicasio Gallego, Antonio de
Capmany, and José María Blanco White. Alcalá Galiano, upon
recalling the early years of the nineteenth century in Madrid, states
that "nobody exceeded Cienfuegos in his love for the tendencies
which were later to be called liberal." He added that Cienfuegos
may have seemed especially extreme in his political ideas, "because
the radicalism in his style implied an equal radicalism in the
content."[20]

As a member of Quintana's circle, it was only natural that Cienfuegos would have had strained relations with the distinguished
dramatist Leandro Fernández de Moratín. Moratín and his colleagues
initially had been rather liberal but they were won over to a more
conservative stance as they acquired support and positions from the
government.[21] As supporters of the government of Godoy whom
they looked to for financial security, Moratín and his friends became
the enemies of Quintana's group, who formed the most radical group
of intellectuals of the Enlightenment. According to Alcalá Galiano,
the ideas of Cienfuegos, Quintana, and their circle of friends were
those of the philosophers of the French Revolution. The hostility
between the groups was not merely political, for it spread to the
literary world. Moratin's group followed the *Principes philosophiques
de la litterature* by Batteux and translated into Spanish by Agustín
García de Arrieta, while Cienfuegos and his friends based their
literary ideas on *Lessons Upon Rhetoric and Belles-Lettres* by the Scots-

man Hugo Blair, a book that had been translated into Spanish by Joseph Luis Muñarriz. In fact, there was no basic difference in the literary theory of these two works. The sharpest conflict of opinion occurred in the appendixes written by the translators or their friends who disagreed in their evaluations of Spanish literature of the Golden Age as opposed to that of the contemporary period. Moratin's circle preferred the earlier epoch, while Quintana's band defended the work of their contemporaries.[22]

Another friend who had an influence upon the thought and poetry of Cienfuegos was a mysterious figure named Florian Coetanfao.[23] A revealing portrait of the relationship between Cienfuegos and Coetanfao can be found in the preface to the tragedy *Idomeneo* that Cienfuegos dedicated to his unknown friend. His effusive declarations of friendship resemble the sentimental prose of the romantic epoch. Although this mysterious figure had, for at least a few years, a strong influence on Cienfuegos's ideology, sentiments, and literary endeavors, no scholar has been able to discover the exact identity of Florian Coetanfao. Menéndez Pelayo, intrigued by the mystery, attempted to identify Coetanfao, tentatively concluding that he was a Spanish revolutionary who lived in Paris during the period of the Directory.[24]

A major theme of the eighteenth century was friendship, and Cienfuegos exemplifies the great importance given it during the Age of the Enlightenment.[25] His deeply felt friendship for Meléndez Valdés, Quintana, and Coetanfao was equaled by the profound affection he expressed for his female friends. One of the closest was the marchioness of Fuerte-Híjar, a passionate lover of literature and a dedicated believer in the Enlightenment ideals of progress, virtue, and universal brotherhood. Cienfuegos dedicated to her a tragedy, *La condesa de Castilla* (The countess of Castile), and a poem, "La escuela del sepulcro" (The graveyard school). The dedication of *The Countess of Castile* reveals her role in the creation of the play and Cienfuegos's great affection for her and her husband. Her husband, the marquis of Fuerte-Híjar, Cienfuegos's friend and protector, founded and became in 1789 the first director of the Royal Economic Society of Valladolid, and after moving to Madrid he was active in the Economic Society, the Order of Carlos III, and the king's council. In 1802 Godoy named him the subdirector of the theaters. Some of Cienfuegos's plays were staged in private theaters including that of the marchioness.[26] Cienfuegos also participated in the literary circle of the duchess of Alba, which included preeminent literary and artistic figures like Jovellanos, Meléndez, Quintana, Somoza, and Goya.

Cienfuegos's poetry affirms his love for various unknown women. Of course, some of these amatory verses appear to be merely formulistic since he wrote them in the fashionable anacreontic style. Others convey the feeling of true love. One of the most passionate declarations of love is to Celima, a woman whose identity is now lost, in his dedication of the tragedy *Zoraida*. An emotional unburdening representative of his excessively sentimental prose, Cienfuegos's regret over the termination of his relationship with Celima underlines his failure to maintain a permanent relationship with any woman. He reveals a similar experience in the poem "Un amante al partir su amada" (A lover on the departure of his beloved). Cienfuegos also laments his failure to achieve a permanent love in a poem entitled "La primavera" (Spring).

Literary and Political Career

From the evidence available, Cienfuegos's first literary publication was to be an edition of the poetry of Fernando de Herrera. In 1785 Cienfuegos and Juan de Peñalver, cadet of the royal guard, applied and obtained permission from the Council of Castile to reedit the poetry of Herrera. Apparently they never carried through with their project because there is no notice of their work being published. Cienfuegos's interest in this poet demonstrates once again the importance given during the neoclassical period to the national literature and history, contradicting the opinion of some historians who perceive neoclassicism as a totally foreign implant. In addition, his interest in the Renaissance poet is significant because, like Cienfuegos, Herrera was an innovative poet introducing new words, taking liberty with the syntax, and expressing himself in a highly emotional tone.

Cienfuegos, Juan Meléndez Valdés, Juan de Peñalver, Diego Clemencín, Ramon Pérez Campos, and Domingo García Fernández applied for permission to publish *El Académico*, a weekly that was to deal with all branches of human knowledge. Their request and a prospectus went to the governor of the Council of Castile on 2 July 1793, and on the twenty-ninth of that month the petitioners were told that they had to prepare and present in advance sufficient material for one year's publication. This, in effect, was a refusal of their application.[27] The prudently written application attests to the difficulties that the adherents of the Enlightenment experienced in the years following the French Revolution. Among other concessions, the editors declared they would not treat certain subjects. It is clear, however, that the publication was to be a voice of the ideology and spirit of the Enlightenment, for in the application the authors declared their love of progress and the sciences. Apparently the request was not sufficiently moderate to allay the fears of the enemies of change, since the weekly never appeared in print.

Cienfuegos also failed in his attempt to gain approval for a translation of Fenelon's didactic narrative *The Adventures of Telemachus*. In his proposal, presented to Godoy in a letter dated 12 May 1796, Cienfuegos deplored bad translations that either "mutilated the meaning and the soul of the original or disfigured its energy, its grace, its color."[28] In the margin of Cienfuegos's application for financial support Godoy denied the request with a brief comment that Covarrubias had already done it. Cienfuegos was probably unaware of this translation, because it was not printed until 1797–98, when it appeared in a two-volume edition. Cienfuegos also failed in his attempt to attain the position of chief librarian of the Reales Estudios de San Isidro.[29] In September of 1798, he applied for the position stating, among other things, that he had acquired knowledge of both Eastern and Western languages with the goal of writing an etymological, analytical dictionary of Spanish, for which he had already prepared considerable material, a comparative Castilian grammar, and a treatise on synonyms. A year later the king selected from among the many applicants the minor poet José Villarroel.

Nonetheless, Cienfuegos did have some success in his search for employment and influence in the capital. For example, the poet and novelist José Mor de Fuentes reports that in 1796 he gave Cienfuegos a collection of poetry which the latter "published with some opportune improvements, at the Royal Printing Press."[30] In 1797 Cienfuegos became a member of the Real Sociedad Económica Matritense de Amigos del País and was also named honorary official of the Ministry of State without salary. The following year the Imprenta Real published a volume containing his poetry and dramatic works, and he was named to head two official publications, the *Gaceta de Madrid* and the *Mercurio de España*, under the aegis of the Ministry of State. Cienfuegos obviously realized the necessity of remaining circumspect in order not to weaken his position, because he removed his most revolutionary poem, "En alabanza de un carpintero llamado Alfonso" (In praise of a carpenter named Alfonso), from the edition of his works that appeared in 1798. He maintained the dual editorship until 1803 when he rose to a higher position in the Ministry of State. Cienfuegos rose rather rapidly through the bureaucratic ranks, and by April 1808, a month before the uprising against the troops of Napoleon, he was receiving a handsome salary of 35,000 reals per year.

His poetry and theatrical works, published by the Imprenta Real in 1798, achieved considerable acclaim. Jovellanos, for example, described his poems as "sublime, tender, and announcing great promise."[31] Cienfuegos's successful literary efforts resulted in his being elected to the Real Academia de la Lengua, becoming a member of that august body in 1799 at the age of thirty-five. Significantly, his most successful play *Zoraida* had had its premiere on 28 June 1798 at the Caños de Peral Theater shortly before his election to the Royal Academy. His tragedy *Idomeneo* had been staged several years earlier in 1792 at the Príncipe Theater. *The Countess of Castile*, although written by 1798, did not receive its first public production until 23 April 1803 in Madrid. In addition, there were readings of performances of his works at the private theaters of Madrid like that of the marchioness of Fuerte-Híjar. Thus Cienfuegos had earned considerable renown as a poet and dramatist before his election to the Royal Academy.

Perhaps a crucial event in his acceptance into the Academy was his submission of the tragedy *Pítaco* in a poetic contest sponsored by the Academy in 1799. The jury did not select a winner, but recognized the merits of *Pítaco* by including it among the three finalists.[32] Perhaps *Pítaco* was too revolutionary to have won the prize, as Marcelino Menéndez Pelayo stated. However, in recompense for not awarding *Pítaco* the prize, this conservative critic believed that the Academy opened its doors to its author.[33] In September of 1799 Cienfuegos applied for membership to the Academy, and at the meeting of 19 September of that same year, presided over by the marquis of Santa Cruz, he was elected to the Academy. On 24 October 1799 he gave the discourse required of new members; his subject was the progress of languages.[34] During the following two years Cienfuegos frequently attended the Academy's meetings and participated in its functions. From 1803 to 1805, however, he attended very few meetings, and from 1806 to 1808 his name does not appear in the notes of the meetings.

Among his contributions to the Academy was his speech delivered on 5 November 1802 to honor the deceased marquis of Santa Cruz. This eulogy for the former president of the Academy was printed in Madrid in 1802. This speech and his eulogy of Joseph Almarza are testimonials of the spirit of the age that glorify the deceased men for their humanitarian ideals, their desire for educational and economic progress, their efforts to better the lot of their countrymen through useful contributions to the nation, and their love of learning, truth, and order.

From 1803 until his death Cienfuegos reduced his activities at the Academy and in fact seldom went there, probably due to his added responsibilities at the Ministry of State, where he was appointed to fill a vacancy in December 1802. He also retained some responsibilities with *Mercurio de España* and *Gaceta de Madrid*. It is possible that the illness, probably tuberculosis, that eventually caused his death began to weaken him so that he had to reduce his activities. Whatever the reasons, Cienfuegos participated much less in the activities of the Academy and the final session of the Academy attended was that of 29 January 1805. In 1804 he was promoted one rank higher at the Ministry of State, and in successive years he rose in rank until he achieved his final post as a fourth officer with a salary of 35,000 reals per year, which was a substantial salary for the time.[35]

Final Days

In February of 1808 Carlos IV signed a decree nominating Cienfuegos to be a knight of the Order of Carlos III. Entrance into this Order required proof of nobility. Suitable testimony was obtained and sent to the officer in charge, who at that time was Cienfuegos's good friend the marquis of Fuerte-Híjar. On 8 April 1808, Fuerte-Híjar gave a decision in favor of Cienfuegos's admission, and on 2 May (the day the citizens of Madrid rebelled against Napoleon's troops in the streets of the capital) the assembly of the Order of Carlos III gathered in the formal meeting gave definitive approval for his admission.

On 2 May 1808, Cienfuegos was bedridden but continued to

direct the affairs of the *Gaceta*, maintaining close communication with the chief editor, Diego Clemencín, who visited him frequently. Since Fernando VII had departed Madrid on 10 April 1808, en route to his exile in France, the *Gaceta* had published articles describing the fervent reception he received from his fellow citizens. Spaniards were demonstrating their patriotism through their support of the young man recently proclaimed king. Thus it was not surprising that on 2 May, while he could hear shooting in the streets, Cienfuegos ordered Clemencín to publish in the *Gaceta* a report from Reus dated 23 April on the proclamation of Fernando VII as king of Spain.

This report in support of the king, which appeared only one day after the uprising in Madrid, was clearly an act of defiance toward the French. The head of the French army of occupation, General Murat, reacted to the uprising with a violent repression of the people of Madrid. Furious with the *Gaceta* and its director, Murat ordered Cienfuegos to report to him immediately, but the chief editor, Clemencín, went instead, because of Cienfuegos's serious illness. Clemencín explained to the irate Frenchman that nothing was published in the *Gaceta* without the official approval of the Ministry of State. Murat commanded him to produce the order to print the news of the proclamation of Fernando as the king of Spain within the hour or he would be shot. Despite his ill health, Cienfuegos had to face General Murat, who harshly reprimanded him and threatened to have him shot if he did not print a correction in the following day's edition. Ignoring the threat upon his life, Cienfuegos refused, and on 4 May he resigned rather than retract the news report. His resignation addressed to the minister of state read: "Not being able to continue serving as officer of the Ministry of State without harm to and loss of my honor and good name, I see myself obliged to resign from that position without there being any possible way for me to continue in it even though it might cost me my life. I hope that your excellency will inform the Council of Government so that it may do what is suitable and authorize whomever they please to supervise the *Gazette*."[36] Quintana expressed the impact of Cienfuegos's patriotism at this critical moment in Spain's history in the prologue to the 1827 edition of *Poesías*, which he dedicated to Cienfuegos. His expression of praise and gratitude for Cienfuegos's brave refusal to bow before the tyrant reveals the esteem in which Cienfuegos was held by his contemporaries.

The repudiation of Murat's order would have meant almost certain death for Cienfuegos had his colleagues at the Ministry not acted in concert on his behalf, also presenting their resignations. On 4 May their spokesmen, Diego Porlier and Narciso de Heredia, went before the Council of Government presided over by Murat, who had assumed total power that very day. When Porlier announced the mass resignation, Murat reacted violently. Nevertheless, the members of the Council, drawing courage from the attitude of Cienfuegos and his colleagues, demonstrated their fortitude by refusing to accept the resignations and in so doing collaborated with them in their defense of Cienfuegos. Murat, who wished to control the Council of Ministers, withdrew his threat to take Cienfuegos's life.[37]

The resignation of Cienfuegos was not accepted; instead, he was granted two months' leave of absence, apparently a compromise to satisfy both Murat and the Council. When the time of the furlough had elapsed, Cienfuegos made a request dated 4 July for another two months' absence from work because he had been ordered to take baths and mineral water as a cure for his ill health. This treatment required Cienfuegos to leave Madrid, but it is not known whether or not he did. He did return to his position at the Ministry in August when Joseph Bonaparte and his army left Madrid. The departure of the army of occupation, which was brought about by the news of the French defeat at Bailén, caused great rejoicing in the streets of Madrid. On 24 September 1808, an assembly of representatives presided over by Floridablanca gathered in Aranjuez to swear fidelity to Fernando VII. The following month a government was formed, but Napoleon Bonaparte then formed an army that retook Madrid in December of 1808.

Most Spaniards involved with the anti-French movement departed a few days before the French army entered Madrid. The officials of the Ministry of State and writers like Quintana who supported independence fled with the leaders of the recently formed government. Cienfuegos, however, remained in the capital most likely because his illness was worsening.[38] This decision, of course, placed him in grave danger. He was in Madrid in December of 1808 when Napoleon demanded that every citizen sign an oath of loyalty to his brother Joseph and ordered justices of the peace to go from house to house securing signatures. Under these circumstances the French did succeed in forcing Cienfuegos to sign the oath on his sick bed. However, an oath signed under such coercion did not reflect the

attitude of the fatally ill poet, who was absolutely opposed to the
Napoleonic invasion and did not accept the authority of King Joseph
Bonaparte. Joseph issued a decree on 25 February 1809 demanding
that all government officials swear their allegiance within three days.
Cienfuegos refused to comply and was dismissed.[39] Joseph Bonaparte
ordered all supporters and associates of the independent government
to be punished. The *Semanario Patriótico*, an organ of the independent
government in Seville directed by Quintana, printed the news of
the arrest of Cienfuegos and others in its number of 8 June 1809.[40]

It was not long before Cienfuegos learned his fate at the hands
of the conquerors whom he called the "vandals of the Seine." Quintana reveals that his sentence was exile in the condition of a hostage.[41]
Cienfuegos refused to beg for a change in the sentence, which he
received without a trial, even though he must have suspected that
his body could not withstand the trip. He must have been consoled
somewhat by having among his fellow prisoners his good friend the
marquis of Fuerte-Hijar. After several days of travel the prisoners
arrived in Orthez in the south of France on 27 June. Cienfuegos
was placed in the home of the businessman Martin Darie, and he
died there three days later, on 30 June 1809. The trip from Madrid
was obviously too demanding for the poet, whose lengthy illness
had left him unable to withstand the rigors of a journey. He was
buried in the cemetery of Orthez, but the exact location is not
known.

Nicasio Alvarez de Cienfuegos accomplished much during his
forty-five years despite his humble beginnings. He became a major
poet of his time and, through his defiance of General Murat, a
memorable figure in the annals of the patriotic struggle to throw
off the yoke of Napoleonic oppression.[42]

Chapter Two

The Early Poems

The Salamancan School

The earliest poetry by Cienfuegos now available was written during his student days at the University of Salamanca and reflects the style of a group of poets called the Salamancan School.[1] This group of poets may be considered the second school of Salamanca, since in the sixteenth century there had been a similar poetic group. A definite affinity exists between the two schools because of the interest and respect that the eighteenth-century poets had for Fray Luis de León and other illustrious predecessors of the sixteenth century. Three leaders of the modern school, the clerics Juan Fernández de Rojas, Diego Tadeo González, and Andrés del Corral, belonged to the same Order of Augustinians that Fray Luis de Leon had. Among renowned figures of the group were José Cadalso, who is given credit for initiating the movement in Salamanca in the early 1770s; and the most distinguished lyric poet of the century, Juan Meléndez Valdés, who first enrolled in the University of Salamanca in 1772, ten years before his disciple Cienfuegos. The latter and his friend Manuel José Quintana are also associated with the Salamanca School despite being considerably younger. Meléndez Valdés, who took Cienfuegos into his literary circle, must have exerted considerable literary and ideological influence upon him.

The poets of the Salamanca School were adherents of the tenets of neoclassicism and, therefore, strong defenders of the dictum that literature should both teach and please, that is, the Horatian *utile dulci*. Looking to the great writers of the sixteenth and seventeenth centuries for inspiration, they sought models among those who also were admirers of the classical tradition. Thus the influence of Garcilaso de la Vega and Fray Luis de León is at least as significant as that of Horace, Anacreon, Sappho, and other poets of Greece and Rome.

Fray Diego González, one of the primary figures of the Salamancan group because of his early contributions to style and themes, and a great admirer of the poetry of sixteenth-century Spain, employed the *lira* that Garcilaso had introduced and Fray Luis de León later refined.[2] There is an obvious link between Fray Luis de León, Fray Diego González, and their disciple Juan Meléndez Valdés. In turn, Cienfuegos, a friend and protégé of Melendez Valdés, could not help but absorb the spirit of the classical tradition as inherited from the Spanish Renaissance poets. In addition to the classical influence, there developed an interest in purely national forms. Meléndez Valdés is credited with the rebirth of the romance, and Cienfuegos wrote at least one romance during his student days in Salamanca. Cienfuegos's verse follow the development in form and themes from narrowly neoclassical to broader, more European and subjective styles characteristic of the poets of the Salamancan School.

While some historians of Spanish literature have viewed eighteenth-century Spanish neoclassicism as dominated by foreign influences, particularly French, Spanish neoclassicists often found inspiration in the literature, history, and legends of their own country. Also characteristic of the Salamancan School was a tendency away from the formulas of neoclassicism toward a receptivity of contemporary philosophical and societal innovations. As a result, the poetry of this school is quite diverse in tone, ranging from the sensual, bucolic anacreontic verses to a melancholic, sentimental vision that hints of the romantic era to come, and even a poetry with a deeply felt social commitment.

An important aspect of the poetry of the Salamancan School is the emphasis on the pastoral. An obvious, although simplistic, indication of this interest in the pastoral mode of antiquity resulted in the use of Arcadian names by many neoclassical writers. Thus it is not unusual to see in the verses of the Salamancan School references to Batilo (Juan Meléndez Valdés), Arcadio (José Iglesias de la Casa), Delio (Diego Tadeo González), Liseno (Juan Fernández de Rojas), Andrenio (Andrés del Corral), and Amintas (Juan Pablo Forner), all of whom were at one time or another active participants in the rebirth of poetry in Salamanca prior to and during the period Cienfuegos spent at the university. Adoption of pastoral names evinces a desire for a more intimate relationship with nature, which with time developed into a union of the poet with nature. The use of figurative language to attribute to nature the feelings of man became a trait of the poetry of the turn of the century.

Diversiones

This collection of youthful verse is important for its revelation of Cienfuegos's beginnings as a poet and its contribution to our understanding of the poets of Salamanca. The manuscript remained unedited until 1968 when the Italian Hispanist Rinaldo Froldi published it.[3] A year later José Luis Cano included these poems in his edition of Cienfuegos's poetry.[4] The title of the collection, *Diversiones* (Diversions), recalls the *Ocios de mi juventud* (Pastimes of my youth) of Cadalso and the anacreontic poetry of Meléndez Valdés, who described his poems as "deliciosos pasatiempos" (delicious pastimes).[5] Cienfuegos wrote these early poems while a university student associated with the dominant poetic group in Spain. A favorite mode of this Salamancan School was the anacreontic and pastoral poetry portraying an artificial setting of lovers, shepherds, soft winds, pleasant streams, and lush fields of flowers. Cienfuegos closely followed this style, and the collection of early poems contains numerous examples of phrases and images that had become commonplace among the Salamancan poets.

Anacreontic poetry of the eighteenth century, brief in form and light in tone, dealt with the joyful themes of wine, women, and song. The poetic world of Anacreon and his followers promotes love and the pursuit of pleasure as the principal expressions of life. These poets developed their hedonistic sensual themes in an idyllic pastoral setting that had its basis in a long literary tradition rather than everyday reality. Their spirit of gallantry was expressed through a search for the most delicate nuances of sensibility and sentiment. The brief and refined anacreontic compositions were a perfect model for poets opposed to the pompous, showy compositions of the baroque era. Ignacio de Luzán, the leading theorist of eighteenth-century Spain, provided a significant impulse to the popularity of Anacreon by translating some of his poems and also citing Anacreon as a perfect example of the humble poetic style ("estilo humilde").[6]

Cienfuegos's collection contains poems of erotic or sentimental themes such as the monostrophe "Anadoris hermosa" (Beautiful Anadoris) and the ballad "Por divertir sus tristezas" (To amuse her sadness). Other poems have descriptive passages that place them in the category of nature poetry, for example, the "Adónicos a la vida del campo" (Adonic verses to life in the country). The unfinished eclogue "La bucólica del Tormes" (The bucolic poem on the river Tormes) celebrates spiritual life in the country, a life whose virtue and peacefulness are unknown to ambitious materialistic individuals whose love is misplaced in worldly goods. A few poems, however, do not fit the pastoral mode of the collection as a whole, including several humorous or satirical epigrams and sonnets (the epigram was not an uncommon form among the poets of Salamanca). The eight brief poems Cienfuegos calls epigrams are witty pieces that follow the classical tradition in their compression, pointedness, clarity, and diversity of themes, which include love, humor, and drunkenness. The most prominent characteristic is their comicality. Two are satires, one of which satirizes a lawyer and the other is an epigram to the same mountaineer whom he mocks in a satirical sonnet.

What is striking about these early poems in general is that already present is a moralistic tone that will appear in Cienfuegos's compositions throughout his literary career. This is evident in his praise of the virtues of country life and of prudence in the "Endecha a los viejos" (Dirge to the elderly) and of poverty in the monostrophe whose opening verse is "El cielo soberano" (The sovereign heavens). But this moralistic tone is more pronounced in the epigrams and sonnets via criticism of society and certain human defects such as the inordinate vanity of the mountaineer, the soldier's distorted sense of military pride, or the ignorance of lawyers. In the bucolic poems, Cienfuegos obviously presents the simplicity of the pastoral life as a contrast to the flaws perceived elsewhere in society. A basic lesson to be taken from these poems of Cienfuegos's youth is that reason is the best guide for life and should control man's actions and passions.

Four sonnets appear in *Diversions,* two of which are satirical while the remaining pair are love poems. The first of the satires, "Soneto a un montañés" (Sonnet to a mountaineer), mocks the man from the northern mountainous region who boasts of his lineage, claiming that his family name surpasses that of the most illustrious nobles of Spain, even the royal Bourbons. He seeks to be honored above Apollo and demands that Apollo's laurels be taken from him, for the arrogant mountaineer wishes to exalt himself with these symbols of fame and honor. The mock heroic tone of these verses concludes with a comic twist:

Pues repita la fama con esmero
desde el uno hasta el otro opuesto polo
que: Viva el Montañés aunque Alojero.

Repeat my fame with care
from one pole to the other:
Long live the Mountaineer Moonshiner!

(P, 195)

The satirical "Soneto a un valiente andaluz" (Sonnet to a valiant Andalusian), like the "Sonnet to a Mountaineer," mocks the boastfulness of a regional type. The Andalusian portrays himself as the most valiant of soldiers. The mocking tone surfaces in the opening line when he declares that he would cut off "his nose and his head" (P, 196) if a better soldier could be found, and asks whether his "crushing sword" was not part of the assault on Rome when that great city surrendered to the Spanish army. But again Cienfuegos ends the sonnet on an absurd note. The Andalusian is reminiscent of the stock comic character of the boastful soldier. Thus, while the soldier is relating his heroic deeds "he sees a mouse, and running wildly, / he shouts repeatedly to arms, to arms / a thousand Moors are chasing me" (P, 196). Clearly the poem fails as a satire because he mocks the haughty Andalusian in a most jejune way. The fearful reaction of the soldier upon seeing a mouse is too far removed from reality, thus destroying the desired satirical effect.

The two love sonnets bear no special titles. In the first, the poet employs traditional imagery such as the sun to magnify the beauty of his beloved Filis. In a lighthearted tone, this sonnet depicts the poet anxiously waiting for his beloved to leave her home certain that her appearance will darken the sun. At last he perceives her descend the staircase, and on seeing her step out into the sunlight,

I remained looking attentively at the sun
and I note, what a rare and prodigious event!
that just as before it continued to shine.

(P, 196)

The second love sonnet has all the cliché-ridden vocabulary of unrequited love; for example, the constant repetition of words expressing rejection such as "desdeñosa," "despreciar," and "condenar." But in the midst of her coldness and disdain the poet sees himself in a favorable light remaining

> . . . always constant
> without my love diminishing
> you prove yourself ungrateful
> and I to be a firm and true lover.
>   (P, 197)

Nothing in this poem suggests that Cienfuegos would become a major poet.

Among the early poems is one romance that describes, unlike the medieval ballads dealing with the heroic deeds of national heroes, the spiritual union of a woman with nature. In this respect the ballad suggests the influence of Meléndez Valdés and reflects the poetic values of the eighteenth century in contrast to those of the romantic poets of the following century, who often wrote ballads whose inspiration can be found in the legends and historical figures of the Middle Ages. The stylized portrait technique of Cienfuegos's other early poems is present here. The troubled female protagonist of the poem reaches out to nature in search of consolation and finds it.

> To relieve her sadness
> the beautiful Cloris went out
> to see the delightful meadow
> one morning in May.
> The gentle tiny goldfinches
> and the soft canaries
> gave her a welcome
> of tender and sweet songs.
>   (P, 191–92)

Adjectives such as soft, tender, and sweet create the mood of gentleness and pleasure in this idealized bucolic world. Although he gives the poem a realistic note by setting it in Salamanca (mentioning the Tormes River that flows by the university city), the poet has idealized nature, all of which desires to please Cloris. Nature is so perfect that

> The restless little fish
> proudly leave the river
> congratulating themselves a thousand times
> for being able to die in that meadow.
> (P, 192)

A common stylistic trait of the bucolic and anacreontic poetry of the epoch, particularly that of Meléndez Valdés, was the use of diminutive forms. Therefore, it is not surprising that Cienfuegos also commonly employed diminutives to give his poems a more tender, delicate note, as with "pececillos" in the above passage. Cienfuegos wrote many poems of this collection in the bucolic mode, including the unfinished "La bucólica del Tormes" (The bucolic poem on the river Tormes). The setting is "the happy springtime," which exemplifies the beauties and fruitfulness of nature. The shepherd Anfiso, in the midst of the rejoicing of gods and nymphs, expresses the ancient *beatus ille* theme. In traditional fashion, he disdains the life of the city with its attendant requirements to court the rich and powerful, preferring the independence of his humble life in the country. The theme, the classical reference, the use of adjectives like "apacibles" and "blando" to idealize nature, are typical of neoclassical pastoral poetry.

The *beatus ille* theme also appears in "Adónicos a la vida del campo" (Adonic verses to the country life), a paean of praise to the pleasures of rural living that extols everything from "The sweet bee / who goes jumping / from branch to branch, / from stalk to stalk," to "a chestnut tree / that gives us its fruit / with an open hand" (*P*, 187–88). The praise of the country life is a common theme of the epoch. Here the tone is joyful and carefree, and lacks the meditative quality of many poems dealing with this theme. But one perceives a sense of melancholy underlying the facade of gaiety that happy nature creates, "if there are sadnessess / we throw them aside" (*P*, 187). This praise of the country life is not a beckoning to the experiences of the real world, but rather to those of an idealized world where the songs of the birds are enchanting and the pleasant fragrance of the beautiful flowers captivates all, the green grass provides a soft cushion to relieve us of our burdens, and the murmuring streams soothe us to sleep. In short, a perfect nature satisfies all our wants. The underlying hedonistic tone of the poem relates it to the anacreontic poetry of the period, which often expressed the classical *carpe diem* theme.

The early poetry contains other common neoclassical themes and forms. "Canción" (Song [*P*, 181–84]) is replete with the clichés of the traditional anacreontic poetry in its description of Cupid as a spirited young man with the power to enchain the haughtiest of spirits. The use of the diminutive form to refer to Cupid ("Cupi-

dillo", "zagalejo"), characteristic of the bucolic-love poetry of the
period, is also one of the striking qualities of the anacreontic poetry
of Meléndez Valdés. Various critics have suggested the similarity
of this stylistic recourse to the delicate, diminutive forms of rococo
painting and plastic arts.[7] Rococo art characteristically combines
the motif of delicacy with a gentle eroticism. Other clichés of the
anacreontic genre present in "Canción" are the metaphor of the
arrows that subject the victim to love's empire, the standard references to the goddesses and other figures of classical mythology,
the youth's heart described as a fierce volcano, and his struggle with
Cupid. The imagery and language employed are those of a centuries-
long tradition of love poetry. Nothing suggests that the poem is
the expression of a deeply felt passion. Use of the standard names
of neoclassical pastoral poetry suggests that the poet was merely
writing within a formula. The composition does demonstrate Cienfuegos's capacity to create rather complicated stanzas with alternat-
ing heptasyllabic and hendecasyllabic verses with an *a b a b c c*
rhyme scheme, although like all his early efforts it lacks the passion,
power, and sincerity of first-rate lyric poetry.

Not all the poems written during Cienfuegos's student days are
expressions of optimism in an idealized world. "Endecha" (Dirge
[*P,* 189–90]) contains clichés such as the river inhabited by nymphs,
while the delicate stylized quality of this world is captured by the
use of diminutives. This beautiful portrait of nature serves to render
the poet's fate more tragic, for now he laments that his good fortune
has changed and the beauties of nature can only testify to the ecstasy
that preceded his lugubrious tears. The poet's depiction of his present woes, however, does not ring true because the stylized treatment
of nature detracts from the sincerity of his grief. The use of tired
imagery to depict an unconvincing fairy-tale world weakens the
emotional impact of the verses. The reader suspects that this is no
more than a literary exercise.

As a mature poet, Cienfuegos became concerned with the injustices that he observed in society. He attacked the poverty of the
working class as symbolized by the carpenter Alfonso in "En alabanza
de un carpintero llamado Alfonso" (In praise of a carpenter named
Alfonso). These early poetic exercises, however, present themes reminiscent of medieval or baroque literature in their moralistic tone
and underlying defense of the established society. Thus in the first
of two poems entitled "Monóstrofe" (Monostrophe), after listing the

symbols of authority and wealth that heaven has given to kings, cardinals, judges, and other authority figures, he declares the poor are more fortunate because the greatest gifts have been bestowed upon them for they enjoy peace and happiness. Also in "Endecha a los viejos" (Dirge to the elderly) Cienfuegos expresses a traditional message promoting a passive acceptance of life's hardships. Like a priest admonishing his flock, Cienfuegos instructs his readers to seek consolation for their misery in prudence and thus overcome disease and troubles. In his later works this centuries-old Christian message will be replaced by the optimism of the Enlightenment that through reason, humanitarianism, and brotherhood man can solve his problems and create a better life for all men here in this world.

Cienfuegos's first poems are in large part a testimony to the popularity of the neoclassical bucolic poetry. The artificial quality of this world of Cupid, shepherds, and shepherdesses is exemplary of the neoclassical mode, and the compositions seem to have been inspired by literary rather than real experiences. In this respect the poet was creating an imagined world comparable to the actions of aristocrats who played at the role of rustics while living in their elegant "cottages." Today one can capture a hint of this spirit in Aranjuez, one of the royal family's luxurious retreats, where Carlos IV's marble-faced and statue-lined Casita del Labrador still remains on the royal grounds. The popularity of the bucolic poetry during this period can be explained as a poetic manifestation of the aristocratic taste of the period.

Cienfuegos's obvious need to follow the tried and true formulas made his early poems stilted, that is, they reflect the propriety and formality of a novice writing within a tradition. Later Cienfuegos's sensitive nature and individualistic spirit will cause him to break away from the neoclassical mode, rejecting control in his innovative use of language through neologisms and turning against reserve through a more intimate, emotional expression of his sensitivities and values. The transition in attitude in Cienfuegos's poetry corresponds to that of Meléndez Valdés, who "during the 1770s, began to withdraw from a total commitment to neoclassical precepts."[8]

Chapter Three
The Mature Poems
The 1798 Edition: A Polemic

When the first edition of his poetry appeared in 1798, Cienfuegos was already building a reputation as a poet. His friend Quintana reports that his poetic compositions were read in manuscript form and his tragedies *Zoraida* and *La condesa de Castilla* had been staged in private homes.[1] *Zoraida* had also been staged at the Caños de Peral Theater in June and August of 1798. In addition, Cienfuegos had published some of his poems in periodicals.[2]

By 1798, Cienfuegos apparently believed that he had polished his poetic skills sufficiently to warrant the publication of his poetry and plays. Thus, in June of that year appeared the one-volume collection entitled *Poesías de D. Nicasio Alvarez de Cienfuegos.* Two months later, Gaspar Melchor de Jovellanos praised Cienfuegos's compositions in his diary, describing them as "sublime" and "tender."[3] Cienfuegos would not have been able at that time to read Jovellanos's encouraging evaluation of his work. On the other hand, he undoubtedly read the harsh criticism of his book by an anonymous reviewer in the *Diario de Madrid* in December 1798. This critic, who called himself "El Pronosticador," wrote an especially sharp denunciation of the tragedy *The Countess of Castile.*[4] That same month in the *Diario de Madrid* another anonymous critic, using the pseudonym of "El Imparcial," wrote an even harsher attack against Cienfuegos's book, accusing him, among other things, of having copied various minor foreign poets whom he names.[5] A few days later, in the 23 December issue of the *Diario de Madrid,* an anonymous writer who called himself "Ayudantillo de la Falange" defended Cienfuegos without naming him.[6] Cienfuegos's defender, who made extensive use of irony, supports the poet's knowledge and use of foreign works and the introduction of subjects such as politics, moral philosophy, and physics into his poetry. This running debate continued in the 12 January 1799 issue of the *Diario de Madrid* with an attack against "El Imparcial" by one of the periodical's editors. The polemics over Cienfuegos and his book concluded with a defense of Cienfuegos in the 18 and 19 January issues of the same periodical.[7] This writer, who signed his article J. A. C., attacked at great length the review by "El Pronosticador," accusing the latter of being an untalented poet who criticized Cienfuegos's work out of spite to avenge an earlier criticism of his own work. J. A. C. responds one by one to all the "flaws" that "El Pronosticador" had found in *La condesa de Castilla.* Cano believes that the final resounding defense of Cienfuegos in this polemic was undoubtedly written by a good friend of the poet.[8] Possibly this debate over the merits of Cienfuegos's compositions was part of the larger literary and political dispute between the faction led by Leandro Fernández de Moratín and the faction whose members included Cienfuegos and Quintana.

Anacreontic and Other Love Poetry

The poems attributed to Anacreon of Teos, the court poet who wrote on the joys of wine and love in the sixth century B.C., are in fact imitations that appeared around the beginning of the Christian era. Immediately after these poems were published in Paris in 1554, reprints, translations, and imitations appeared throughout Europe. Francisco de Quevedo, apparently the first to translate these supposed poems of Anacreon into Spanish, did so before 1610, but his work remained unpublished until 1794. The Golden Age poet who played the most important role in the development of the anacreontic mode in Spain was Esteban Manuel de Villegas, whose *Eroticas* appeared in 1618. While his elegant verse was admired by his contemporaries, his fame became even greater during the following century when his *Eroticas* was reprinted in 1774 and again in 1797. During the final decades of the eighteenth century and the early years of the following century there was a great burst of enthusiasm for poetry written in the style of Anacreon.

Cienfuegos's interest in the anacreontic genre resulted in translations of four odes by Anacreon. These, like his own original compositions in this genre, deal with the standard themes of love, wine, and song; in short, the enjoyment of sensual pleasures now because it is impossible to stop the rapid passage of time. Love for the anacreontic or rococo poets is a game or jest, not an ardent, all-consuming passion. Nevertheless, these poems did not always de-

scribe the idealized harmony of two lovers; Cienfuegos also depicted
the misfortune of unrequited love as in "Mis transformaciones" (My
transformations). The erotic, joyful anacreontic poetry is a manifestation of that element of eighteenth-century life that strove to be
pagan, a product of a philosophy of life that saw this world as a
positive value and did not reject its pleasures for the sake of a
heavenly reward. In fact, this genre can be interpreted as a criticism
of the deadly earnestness of the intellectuals of the Enlightenment
and may explain Jovellanos's outspoken advice to his friends in
Salamanca to refrain from writing frivolous anacreontic poems in
favor of more serious themes.[9] The popularity of the idyll in the
eighteenth century may also be a reaction to the pressures that society
exerted on the individual. The poet and his reading public could
escape in the idyll to a land of peace and harmony where they felt
a communion with nature.

"Mi destino" (My destiny), the opening poem of Cienfuegos's
collected works, serves as a preface to that collection. The poem's
tone, unlike what the title suggests, is frivolous, presenting a de-
ceptive view of the author's life and works, except for describing
him as humane and compassionate—qualities that were very important to him, for they are manifested constantly in his writings.
His efforts and accomplishments in the literary and political spheres
are, in fact, testimony to the falseness of the hedonistic view expressed in "My Destiny." Here the poet depicts himself as a baby
in his little cradle ("cunita") surrounded by Cupid and a thousand
other cupids ("otros mil amorcitos") who demonstrate their affection
and love for him. One falls asleep beside him after giving him three
kisses. Cupid's conquest of the poet creates for him the destiny of
a lover. Since then his fortune has been "to love Filis passionately
/ until my final breath" (P, 57). "My Destiny" has a musicality
deriving from the brevity of the heptasyllabic verse with its strong
accent on the sixth syllable. Assonance in the even-numbered lines
also adds to the rhythm and regularity of the structure. The simplicity and musicality of the verses enhance the hedonistic tone of
the poem with its portrayal of a magical love and avoidance of
anything that brings to mind the real world. The poet's worldview
expressed in this poem reflects the eighteenth-century attitude that
only that which is joyful and contented is worthy of song. Of course,
another and perhaps more widely recognized side of the Age of
Enlightenment considered meritorious of song only that wisdom

that leads to peace and virtue for the individual and harmony for society. Cienfuegos's major compositons tend to treat these serious, philosophical, and political subjects.

The use of the diminutive forms ("cunita," "amorcitos," "hermanitos," "cerferillo") and the references to classical mythology (Mars, Themis, Cupid, Cytherea) are characteristics of the School of Salamanca. This poem and much of Cienfuegos's early poetry recall the style and mood created by Meléndez Valdés in his anacreontic verse and Cadalso in his collection of poems entitled *Pastimes of My Youth,* as is not unexpected since the anacreontic poets worked within very narrow limits: similar metrical patterns, an air of erotic playfulness, an insistence on the enjoyment of the moment, and denial of all problems. These limitations, particularly the poverty of themes, required considerable skill of the poet. To overcome the boredom created by the similarities of this type of poem, he had to strive for an attractive sound and rhythm in the verse.

"My Transformations," the second poem of his collected poetry, belongs like the first to the anacreontic genre, but its movement and grace make it a superior poem to "My Destiny." In "My Transformations" the poet declares that if he could request any favor from heaven he would not ask for riches, power, or fame but rather that he undergo metamorphoses to win over his beloved Laura. He would be a rose ("rosita") that his love would pick from the valley and place close to her heart, but his glory and hopes would disappear as quickly as the life of a rose passes. Next he dreams of being transformed into a butterfly to attract her:

> She will want to catch me
> and, with quiet steps,
> she will come, I will flee, and flighty,
> I will leave her behind tricked.
> And if the dew dampens
> my tender little wings?
> She follows me, I am lost,
> She seizes me harshly.
> But at least on expiring,
> with a tremulous voice
> I could happily
> tell her: I loved you!
>
> (*P,* 58)

He then imagines that he could be a gentle breeze ("ceferillo") to refresh his beloved when August burns the meadows. But he would cease all these metamorphoses if Laura would love him as he loves her. The poet reveals the torment of unrequited love, saying that he would not exchange the whole world for the happiness of having her love.

The anacreontic themes of the brevity of life and the invitation to sensual pleasures appear in several poems of this collection. "El otoño" (Autumn), for example, depicts the flight of time through the rapid changes of seasons. Bacchus is the most prominent among the pagan gods and goddesses whom the poet evokes, calling him father Bacchus and declaring that "I burn with a violent / bacchic thirst" (P, 112). He commands others to join him in his madness because "pleasures / disappear like smoke leaving in their place / vain memories" (P, 113). Such thoughts depress him so much that like a romantic he sees despair everywhere. His exclamation "Tristeza universal!" ("Universal sadness!") (P, 113) suggests the pessimistic worldview of the romantics.[10]

In "El túmulo" (The tomb) he again meditates on the brevity of life. The theme is that of Anacreon: the decision to enjoy life as a response to the uneasiness created by man's mortality. The poem's structure follows that of Anacreon in that hedonism is presented as a logical reaction to man's situation. Love, as in many of his poems, is viewed as a powerful eternal force. But the principal message of the poem, which is written in the ballad meter and rhyme, is the classical theme of enjoying the rosebuds of youth.

"Precio de una rosa" (The price of a rose) also belongs to the anacreontic love genre. It consists of a clever erotic game based on the changing price of the rose until the lover demands a kiss for each bee in the swarm that circles the flower. This light, frothy poem is written in heptasyllabic verses with assonant rhyme in the even-numbered lines. The rapid flow of the verses contributes to the musicality and enhances the lighthearted tone. Much of the imagery in this clever treatment of the theme of unrequited love recalls that of other love poems, for example, the rose- and pearl-colored cheeks. The image of the butterfly to attract the lover, however, is enhanced by verbs that vividly depict the pursuit of these creatures, who dart suddenly here and there. Likewise, the poet skillfully portrays the image of the breeze softly caressing the beloved. The repetition of *s* captures the sound of the gentle breeze in her face: "yo soplaré en su frente / mis más suaves auras" (*P*, 59).

Another poem of this group is "La despedida" (The leave-taking), which bears a close resemblance to Meléndez's poem of the same title. The separation or leave-taking of lovers became a popular theme among the poets of the epoch. Cienfuegos also treated this theme in his "Oda a Nice" (Ode to Nice) and "Un amante al partir su amada" (A lover on the departure of his beloved). The popularity of this theme among the late eighteenth-century Spanish poets was due in large part to the great popularity of the Italian composer Metastasio, whose aria "Farewell to Nice" (which Meléndez Valdés translated into Spanish) became famous through its numerous renditions in public and private theaters.

The love poetry of Cienfuegos often reveals the soul of a sensitive man with its constant expression of tender emotions. Thus in "El propósito" (The intention) he cannot ignore the tears of a woman, despite her having been untrue to him. Ruled by emotion, he surrenders to her tears and pardons the woman who had mistreated him and will repeat her infidelity in the future.

Cienfuegos was a sensitive man whose emotional revelations may have been intensified by the spirit of the time. Like Shaftesbury and others, he declares in "A un amigo que dudaba de mi amistad" (To a friend who doubted my friendship) that love is a powerful force that controls nature and without it the world turns to chaos and disunity. Everything positive is the product of love, and the lack of love is the equivalent of death. This poem is representative of his major works, which treat questions of man, nature, society, and morality. Cienfuegos is revealed as a sentimentalist who perceives nature in conflict with man because egocentric humanity rejects nature, causing injustice and suffering in society. In his enthusiasm he equates nature and love which produces all that is beautiful and good:

> . . . whatever is grown
> is the offspring of love; all beauty
> all good is love; Nature
> is nothing more than love.
>
> (*P*, 126)

This equation of nature and love is representative of Cienfuegos's poetry, for a basic idea of his worldview is that love is the unifying principle that produces harmony and beauty in the universe. Because of his spiritual interpretation of nature, his poetry often suggests a pantheistic view of the universe. Cienfuegos turned to the goodness and beauty of nature as a consolation because a society without love was chaotic and evil. Nature offered peace and harmony in contrast to an unjust society that rejected the virtuous man. The prominence given to nature is not surprising because a preeminent slogan of the Enlightenment was "Follow nature!," which meant to follow truth. Nature was regarded as the true essence of things, that is, those harmonious laws decreed by God that govern the universe.

Among the autobiographical poems of Cienfuegos is "A Lover on the Departure of His Beloved." The poem is addressed to Laura, the literary name for a lady whose true identity remains hidden. This woman figures in other poems, which are equally vivid accounts of the love relationship. Such intimate revelations, of course, were not unique to Cienfuegos, since others like Cadalso and Meléndez Valdés had written similar confessions. In Cienfuegos's poem, however, there is a movement away from the universal quality of the descriptive passages to a greater realism through references to specific locales in Madrid that still exist.

Again, in "En ausencia de Cloe" (Without Cloe) Cienfuegos departs from the description of an idyllic pastoral nature to a more realistic portrayal of the world. This poem, which was not published until 1816, captures the city of Madrid in the following description of Cloe's home:

> Oh! The torches that in the shadowy night
> illuminated the entrance to her mansion
> are all dead; the doors
> are closed in silent darkness.
>
> (P, 147)

This description is also a metaphor for the relation between the poet and his beloved Cloe, conveying the hopeless situation in which the poet finds himself. For Cloe's love has died like the torches that illumined her home.

Another of Cienfuegos's favorite love themes is that of his sentimental nature making it impossible for him to avoid love. In "El propósito" (The intention), written in the traditional ballad form, he describes his own sentiments in a moment of sadness, declaring his wish to have nothing more to do with love.

In the following poem, "La violación del propósito" (The violation of the intention), the poet again writes subjectively on the same theme. As in romantic poetry, there is a constant egocentric preoccupation:

> I pant, I tremble, my eyes
> burst with fiery tears
> and a thousand fleeing moans
> burn my thirsty lips.
> I am burning, I am burning Laura,
> ....
> Laura, nothing but Laura, Laura
> is my passion, my universe.
>
> (P, 74)

Cienfuegos emphasizes the sentimental motives of the first-person protagonist. The careful analysis of the emotions develops into a highly personal revelation whose subjectivism creates a tone similar to that of romantic peotry.

Two other poems with the theme of the impossibility of not being in love are "El amante desdeñado" (The rejected lover) and "Los amantes enojados" (The angry lovers), wherein Cienfuegos returns to the idealized pastoral setting of his youthful verse. There is, however, a touch of personal experience in his references to the Tormes and Otea rivers of Salamanca that separate the poems from those of purely classical inspiration.

Melancholy

Romantic melancholy is an uneasiness or sadness without a known cause, accompanied by a desire for some nebulous object. The disquietude that results from this sickness produces, paradoxically, a certain pleasure along with the suffering. Cienfuegos expresses this paradox when he combines the sentiments of joy and sadness in "To a Friend Who Doubted My Friendship." Among the many effects of no longer having the friendship of the man who now doubts his love is one which the poet calls "my happy melancholy" ("mi feliz melancolía" [P, 121]).

Cienfuegos often wrote of the sadness in his life, but he invariably provides a specific cause for his melanchoy and an object that will cure his ills. Unfortunate love affairs are one of the major causes of his melancholy. In "La primavera" (Spring) he deplores his fate that he will never be happy. Unlike the richness of nature he sadly contemplates his barren life: "unloved / without children, without a wife / my spring will never be beautiful" (P, 110). In other poems it is not his failure to find true love but the contemplation of death and the rapid passage of time that depress him and cause his melancholy. Cienfuegos does not depict the tormented romantic soul suffering from a constant dissatisfaction with the world.

His failure to create a truly romantic psychology was due to his deeply rooted beliefs in the values of the eighteenth century. The optimism of the Enlightenment had not yet given way to the pessimism of the romantic era. Men still had faith in the power of reason to create a better world. With reason as a guide man could be happy:

> . . . Who on earth
> was ever happy bemoaning evils?
> Reason, reason, is the only path
> that can guide you to joyful virtue
> and to happiness.
>
> (P, 175)

Reason guides one through moderation and prudence to true values and therefore to the attainment of happiness.

Sensibility

The aesthetics of the final decades of the eighteenth century are characterized by a balance between reason and sentiment.[11] The primary literary theory continued to be neoclassicism, but a new aesthetic based on the sensualist philosophy of Locke became more and more important. Locke denied the existence of innate ideas; rather, all knowledge was believed to be acquired gradually through sensorial perception. While Locke admitted a category of reflection that included mental functions, some of his followers, like Condillac, denied all thoughts that were independent of sensorial perception. The effect that these modern theories had on literature was an increasing emphasis on feelings and emotions. Reason alone was seen as no longer sufficient in and of itself; feeling now became an equal partner. The authors of the late eighteenth century, who are sometimes called preromantics, are the product of this rational and sensualist ideology. This emphasis on sensibility can be seen in the promotion by Shaftesbury of an ethical and aesthetic theory based on the sensibility of man. Hutcheson later advanced this theory to the most complete definition of what constituted the model of moral perfection for the Enlightenment, a model that originated in the Greek ideal of beauty and virtue. Among other important aestheticians was Immanuel Kant, who postulates that those who possess the sentiment of the sublime are inclined toward the higher sentiments and therefore have a moral superiority. [12]

The eighteenth-century sensualist philosophy's impact upon the spirit of the age was particularly noticeable in the literary world. Novelists, dramatists, and poets produced many works whose most striking quality is an extraordinary emphasis on the emotions. [13] One example of this phenomenon was the creation of a new dramatic genre called the "comedia lacrimosa" ("lachrymose comedy") in which the dramatist's principal goal appears to have been the creation of the most emotional conflicts and resolutions possible. [14]

The writers of the eighteenth century not only created literary works whose characters were often moved to tears, but they themselves speak of their unrestrained emotions. Meléndez Valdés, for example, after reading a letter from Jovellanos, writes to his friend that "when I read it, I shed countless tears and I was almost unable to sleep all that night, but these tears were more of friendship and love. . . ." [15] In the prologue of the 1797 edition of his poetry, Meléndez Valdés reveals a similar reaction upon reading the works of classical authors.

It is not surprising, therefore, that Cienfuegos also wrote both poetry and prose in a sentimental, lachrymose tone. Like his master Meléndez Valdés, he shed many tears in his verses, as in the poem dedicated "To a Friend Who Doubted My Friendship":

> Goodbye, oh my happy melancholy,
> by wresting now from my eyes
> the tears that I shed, you submerge
> my heart in intense flames and kindle it
> in the volcano of love that devours me.
>
> (*P*, 121)

Cienfuegos here resorts to the traditional metaphors of love poetry in images such as the flames and volcano of love. However, the intensity of the poet's own emotions breaks with the neoclassical tradition. Clearly these verses point to a new era in Spanish poetry. Cienfuegos and others of the Age of Enlightenment are the fore-runners of the romantics, who likewise were not ashamed to weep publicly.

In "La rosa del desierto" (The desert rose) Cienfuegos presents the traditional theme of the rose as a symbol of the fragility of youth and beauty, with the power to calm the jealousy of a lover, renew the ardor of the aged spouse, and soften the heart of the evil man. Cienfuegos adds to the poetic commonplace the tone of the eigh-teenth-century sensibility. Beauty causes tenderness, which in turn produces virtue. Upon seeing the beauty of the rose the passerby "may stop and bless you / and feel and weep like me, and happier / continue along his fortunate path" (P, 152). This portrait of the tearful poet and the poem's moralistic lesson have a counterpart in the tearful comedies of the eighteenth-century drama.

The exalted passion identified with romantic poetry occurs most strikingly in "El rompimiento" (The dispute). The protagonist re-lates his amorous misfortunes in the first person, creating the sub-jectivism associated with romanticism. He resorts to numerous exclamations and rhetorical questions in his emotional outburst upon being rejected by "inconstant Filis." There is considerable self-pity in the relation of his woes, as in the comparison of Filis to a goddess while he is like a "tender, helpless infant." The setting, while reflecting the eighteenth-century concept of the sublime, bears a similarity to romanticism:

> In the cold silence
> of the quiet night,
> in the uncertain ray of the opaque moon.
> (P, 86)

The repeated use of words like treachery and betrayal and the emo-tional outbursts of the distraught protagonist also serve to create the passionate tone of the poem.

A more pathetic poem is "A Galatea, que huyó de su casa por seguir a un amante" (To Galatea who fled her home to follow a lover). The pathos of this poem arises from the situation of a desperate mother whose daughter has abandoned her to accompany a lover. The poem is a lengthy monologue in which the mother, unable to understand her daughter's actions, laments her fate. The poem's tone is perhaps best exemplified when the tearful mother calls upon her dead husband in a moment of pure pathos. The exaggerated effort to evoke pity and sympathy in the reader relates this work to the development of sentimental literature in the eighteenth century.

Cienfuego's poetry suffers at times from unnecessary repetition, a tendency toward bathos, and a rhetorical tone produced by extensive use of questions, exclamations, and elevated declamatory language. Perhaps the most negative qualities of Cienfuegos's style occur in "Ode to Nice," which was inspired by the performance of a work by the Italian composer Metastasio that probably took place at the home of his friend the marchioness of Fuerte-Híjar. The description of the emotional performance of the two lovers, particularly the aria in which Nice's lover leaves her, touches on bathos. There is a lack of restraint in its repetition, exclamations, questions, and elliptical phrases. The poem reaches its irrational emotional peak when the narrator asks, "Where has my bewitched mind lost itself?" (P, 94).

Friendship

Devotion to the ideal of friendship is an outstanding characteristic of the poets of the School of Salamanca. Numerous poems by this group reveal a profound sense of the sacredness and consolation of friendship. Cienfuegos wrote many verses on the noble passion of friendship in the manner that had swept through Europe during the second half of the eighteenth century. The ecstatic enthusiasm and tender love for his friends bear a close relationship to the Platonic love expressed by the poets of the Renaissance. Cienfuegos's concept of friendship is fully evident in the dedication of the 1798 edition of his works. The exalted passion of his words testifies to the ecstasy of his sentiments in the rapturous eulogy of friendship:

> What protection will these humble verses,
> beloved fruit of my soul and faithful expression
> of its sensibility, tenderness and melancholy
> implore? With no other passion than that of
> loving, with no other ambition than that of

being loved, they alone will be my Maecenas
who are able to give me in love the only recompense
that I desire. Who will they be but the delightful
companions of my life, the absolute masters of
my heart, those who, knowing my thoughts,
my inclinations, my passions, my
weaknesses, and even my vices, in turn open their
souls to me so that I may read therein their
friendship and virtues? Oh refuge of my sorrows,
consolation of my afflictions, remedy of my needs,
tutelary gods of the happiness of my life! Oh,
my friends, could I fail to give you a public
testimony of my love and of my gratitude, for if
there is any moral beauty in my poems, I have copied
it all from your beautiful hearts!
Your intimate friendship has taught me indulgence,
diligence, compassion, sincerity, truthfulness,
tenderness, generosity, the giving of oneself,
and so many and so precious virtues as shine so
eminently in you and, incapable of imitating them,
I am content to publish them with all the enthusiasm
of my admiration and gratitude.

                                        (P, 51–52)

The importance of this preface is its emphasis on the intimacy of
the relationship between Cienfuegos and his friends. The manner
in which Cienfuegos describes his friendships is not surprising because the poets of Salamanca considered it to be the principal way
to achieve virtue; in fact, the ardent expressions of friendship
throughout the period demonstrate that it was one of the highest
ideals of the Age of Enlightenment. The sincerity with which these
poets wrote on this theme is important to consider when reading
the bucolic and anacreontic poetry of the time. The writers of this
age apparently moved with ease from the idealized world of the
shepherd to the most profound and intimate themes.

Cienfuegos added a new dimension to the poetry of his epoch by
writing verses on female friendship, a topic strangely absent from
the works of other poets. One of his best friends, as noted in chapter
1, was the marchioness of Fuerte-Híjar. He not only dedicated to
her a play, *The Countess of Castile,* but also a poem, "La escuela del
sepulcro" (The graveyard school) in which a friend expresses her

love to the marchioness, thus demonstrating that the affection experienced in life can also be shared in death.

Among the characteristics of romanticism was nostalgia, and desire to relive the past appears in the poetry of Cienfuegos. In "El recuerdo de mi adolescencia" (Memory of my youth) he looks back on the friendships of his days in Salamanca and is saddened by the realization that those days will never return. In his recollection of the past he resorts to the ancient *ubi sunt* theme:

> Where are you beloved companions
> of my youth? Where will I
> follow you so that I may find
> simple friendship, old pleasures
> and smiling, virtuous tranquillity?
> It's gone, it's gone, they answer.
>
> (*P*, 129)

Like Rousseau, Cienfuegos views society pessimistically. He sees a diseased world in which man appears unable to avoid being corrupted. In his desire to escape the evils of his surroundings, Cienfuegos can only look to the past, particularly those idyllic days with his friends which he describes in "Memory of My Youth."

The fervor and desolation of "Spring" suggest the spirit and tone of romanticism. The poet decries his fate upon observing the fruitfulness and joy of spring in contrast to his own barren, unfortunate life. The alienated poet's melancholic preoccupation with his own emotions prefigures a characteristic of nineteenth-century romantic poetry. In "Autumn," however, self-pity caused by the poet's isolation is assuaged by the love of his friends. Here he describes his melancholy in terms reminiscent of romanticism. Alone in the world he looks about him and depressed by his dire pessimism, he cries out against life, perceiving sadness everywhere ("¡Tristeza universal!" [*P*, 113]). But his suffering will be remedied by the arrival of his friends. This poetic eulogy of friendship ends on an egocentric note when he identifies himself by name, a trait of Cienfuegos's prose and verse.

Again, in "Mi paseo solitario de primavera" (My solitary spring walk), his only source of hope and consolation is the affection of friends. He condemns man for rejecting the love that makes men brothers for the sake of riches, idle pleasures, false honor, and fame

that divide rather than unite mankind. In the following verses he
expreses a cliché of the Age of Enlightenment, that the loss of reason
produces evil:[16]

> His reason clouded over, in his breast
> his heart expired; in his blinded mind
> he forged new idols. . . .
>
> (P, 118)

Man's failure to recognize that friendship is the source of virtue and
happiness results in evil:

> Oh, Oh! outside of you there is no universe
> for this friend who breathes because of you.
> Perhaps one day august friendship
> will unite souls throughout the wide world
> in fraternal bond. Oh! no, my eyes
> asleep in eternal night
> will not see such a great good. But, meanwhile
> love me, my friends, and my tender heart
> will repay your love, and till my death
> I will seek my happiness in your hearts.
>
> (P, 120)

There is a note of pessimism in these verses as the poet recognizes
that he will not live to see universal brotherhood. Nevertheless, he
creates a personal realm of intimate friends who are able to shelter
themselves from the world. The poem's implied goal is, however,
to change the world to correspond to the ideal attained by the poet
and his friends.

One of his major statements on the theme of friendship occurs
in "To a Friend Who Doubted My Friendship" where he credits
love with being the source of life and all that is good. It is significant
that this love is that of friends, for earlier in the poem he disparaged
marriage for its lack of disinterested love. The exalted feelings that
he experiences on contemplating the blessing of his friendships and
the mixture of tears and happiness capture the tone of the late
eighteenth-century sentimental literature.

The theme of friendship was not unique to Cienfuegos, but he
probably treated it with greater fervor and in a more personal manner

than most other authors of the time. Cienfuegos credits friendship with qualities that transcend those usually attributed to it. In his view the fraternal bond of friendship is a powerful union that not only conquers death but also creates happiness, virtue, and even civilization itself. The warm affection for one's friends as an essential quality in a civilized, harmonious society was one of the most typical concepts of eighteenth-century Spanish literature.

Currency of the theme in Spain was most likely due to the popularity of Jean-Jacques Rousseau and Solomon Gessner, both of whom were well known in the Iberian peninsula.[17] The intense focus on friendship in the eighteenth century was not a mere coincidence.[18] Spanish society changed drastically during the Age of Enlightenment, and one of the more dramatic alterations occurrred in the attitudes toward marriage. Matrimony suffered a marked loss of prestige as evidenced by a diminishing number of marriages.[19] According to Carmen Martín Gaite, the idealistic motives for choosing a partner had virtually disappeared, and marriage was now "conceived openly as a business."[20] Cienfuegos inveighs against the institution of marriage with bitter invective.

Cienfuegos's tender expressions of affection for his friends are as excessive to the modern reader as they were to some readers of his own time. For example, José Gómez Hermosilla, a critic of the neoclassical tradition, faulted Cienfuegos for the affectation of his sensibility. The critic Hermosilla mocked Cienfuegos's declarations of passionate friendship and questioned the sincerity of the poet's sentiments.[21] Hermosilla considered unusual metaphors and language to be improper and pedantic. For example, he considered Cienfuegos's request for "cariños" improper because of its literal meaning of "kisses" or "caresses." Later in the nineteenth century, Marcelino Menéndez Pelayo also found shortcomings in Cienfuegos's verses because of their excessive sentimentality and the affectation in his treatment of friendship.[22]

Despite their exaggerated tone, Cienfuegos's fiery declarations of friendship, which do seem affected and false to the modern ear, must have been the sincere expressions of a sentimental man. The fact that he wrote so often in both prose and verse on the theme of friendship is evidence of his sincerity. It is highly doubtful that he was merely imitating a theme that had attained popularity throughout Europe and been adopted by other Spanish writers. José Luis

Cano has stated, "It is evident that he exaggerated his sentiments
rhetorically as every poet is wont to do; but it doesn't seem credible
that he would sing what he didn't feel as Hermosilla claimed.[23]

Death

The theme of death appears often in the poetry of Cienfuegos,
and some influence of the prose and verse compositions of José
Cadalso is apparent in "En la ausencia de Cloe" (The absence of
Cloe), where death in the company of the beloved becomes an
expression of love. The poet declares his hope that

> One day, one hour, one instant
> together in an embrace,
> her lips and eyes in mine,
> My breast and heart next to hers
> may we die! May one tomb,
> may one single pious coffin enclose
> our ashes in eternal rest!
>
> (P, 148)

The romantic tone of these verses is not a typical Cienfuegos presentation of the theme of death. Like Edward Young, the author
of *Night Thoughts,* his poems on death usually have a more general
moralizing tone.

In the ballad "El Cayado" (The shepherd's walking stick), an old
shepherd through a dialogue with an ash tree contemplates the
inevitability of death. The protagonist meditates on the principal
stages of life relating them to the changes in the world about him:

> I note sad changes
> wherever my eyes turn
> everything is strange to me
> and abandons me in my old age.
>
> (P, 77)

He seeks identification with the unchanging ash tree:

> Ash, my friend, death
> which pardons no one
> because dying is unavoidable,

> rapidly approaches me.
> Would that, when the end arrives,
> for my final glory,
> some pious man put
> my bones at your feet.
>
> (*P, 79*)

Appropriately the poem ends with the onset of night as the old man finishes his meditation on the passage of time and humanity's inevitable fate. The poem demonstrates Cienfuegos's tendency to moralize: "And the sun is not more beautiful / than virtuous old age" (*P, 75*). Another characteristic of his poetry found here is the emotional emphatic style, with numerous exclamations and imperatives that are often repeated ("Leave . . . leave;" "Come . . . Come") and apostrophes ("Oh, time, time!").

In contrast to the positive view of mankind of many poems is the epistle "A Mi amigo, en la muerte de un hermano" (To my friend on the death of a brother) which focuses on the tragic aspects of life. The writer on the faults of mankind concludes that death is, in fact, a happy release from the misery and evil of this world, which is pictured as a vale of sorrows, suffering, and scandal. The destructive effects of evil, injustice, and misuse of authority induce the poet's nightmarish vision of life:

> Horrid wasteland of burning sand
> where, midst universal aridity and death
> perhaps a solitary bush
> exerts itself to bloom: such is the image
> of this cruel life that we love so much.
>
> (*P, 138*)

The theme of death appears in several other poems. Among them is "In Praise of a Carpenter Named Alfonso," with a moralistic lesson similar to that of "The Graveyard School." In "Autumn" the poet speaks of his own death and burial. Friendship motivates him to speak of his own death in "To the Marquis of Fuerte-Híjar" where he expresses a desire for the solitude of the grave in order to avoid having to witness the aging and death of his friend.

This morbid preoccupation with death reaches its culmination in one of Cienfuegos's longest poems "The Graveyard School," which consists of three hundred and four hendecasyllables. The title aptly describes the content of this poem in which the poet uses many traditional conventions such as the *ubi sunt* theme. A more objective point of view is achieved as the poet does not intervene directly through the use of the first person. The lugubrious, melancholic tone of this poem and its general moralistic approach suggest the influence of the English poet Edward Young. Addressed to the poet's friend the marchioness de Fuerte-Híjar, in an effort to console her upon the death of her friend the marchioness de las Mercedes, the poem resembles romantic poetry in its presentation of the themes of death, solitude, and melancholy, and in its nocturnal setting:

> the quiet night
> encloses the mortals in its shadow,
> and quiets the world that lies tranquil
> submerged in a sea of silence.
>
> (P, 168)

But her tears for the friend who lies imprisoned in the coffin disturb the silent calm. The light of flickering candles emphasizes the melodramatic and lugubrious setting. Cienfuegos leads us through a vast cemetery while conjuring up the melancholic voices of the dead. Melancholic reverie on the power and inevitability of death provides a moralistic lesson on the emptiness of the glories of this world. "The Graveyard School" teaches man to consider the brevity of life, which is described as "Only a wink, by turning your face / you will see your death touching your birth" (P, 174). Man should avoid error for it is a moral fault: "error is an evil" (P, 175). Invoking the corpse, Cienfuegos warns us to lead a better life, for the glory and pleasures of this world are fleeting. The poem recalls the traditional Christian view of mortal man as opposed to the hedonism of the anacreontic genre, with its call to sensual pleasures. Cienfuegos's poetry thus expresses a peculiar blend of opposing views. He juxtaposes the hedonism of the carpe diem theme with the Christian view of this life as a preparation for the next from the perspective of a humanitarian committed to reform and progress.

Social Poetry

Cienfuegos represents very well the two principal aspects of the literature of the Enlightenment: the intense emotion of the sensitive man and the reformer's zealous concern for mankind. These are often combined in his humanitarian and revolutionary poems in which he advocates the ideals of the age: equality, brotherhood, love of virtue, and progress. These verses dedicated to reforming society reveal a sensitive poet moved by his love for humanity.[24] Cienfuegos's social poems, as a reflection of the spirit of the Enlightenment, contain similarities with the ideology of writers like Rousseau, whose works were well known in Spain.[25] Cienfuegos was not the first in Spain to write poetry promoting the ideology of the Enlightenment. Earlier Jovellanos and Meléndez Valdés had composed verses on humanitarianism, universal brotherhood, virtue, and similar themes. Cienfuegos, likewise, turned to poetry to express his outrage against social injustice and the economic disparity between the rich and poor. As a government functionary, Cienfuegos's hesitancy to appear radical led to the fact that his most revolutionary poem "In Praise of a Carpenter Named Alfonso" was not included in the 1798 edition of his poetry.

A testimony of Cienfuegos's psychological state at this time in his life is a poem which is a reminiscence of the joys of his youth in Salamanca. "Memory of My Youth," addressed to Batilo, the poetic name of Meléndez Valdés, expresses the poet's disillusionment with his fellowman and the world after his arrival in Madrid. In contrast to this bitter outburst, which undoubtedly resulted from the disappointment of his life in the capital and what he saw as the flagrant self-interest of others, was the recollection of the idealistic humanitarianism, "Sweet equality of brotherly love" (*P*, 128), of his friends in Salamanca. It is not surprising to see this emphasis on friendship, for among the poets of Salamanca it was a most noble passion and the principal means of achieving virtue. This spirit of friendship contrasted to his experience in Madrid where be became saddened by an urban society which brought out the egoism innate in all men. In the capital he observed a more materialistic society where men gained satisfaction in outshining others. Also, in the anonymity of a metropolis, one could appear to be other than what one was. The conspicuous consumption created by burgeoning commerce and urbanization, and satirized in the *sainetes* of Ramon de la Cruz, produced vain and avaricious men.

Cienfuegos, who believed that the active promotion of the public good held society together against the force of egoistic men, lamented what he observed in Madrid. Unlike those who acted only in their self-interest, he believed that it was the duty of men as citizens to act according to the public interest and as moral beings to behave in agreement with the demands of virtue. Despite his disillusionment with life in Madrid, he was able to find solace in the friendship of writers, artists, and others who congregated at the home of the duchess of Alba (Meléndez Valdés, Goya, the marquis and marchioness of Fuerte-Híjar, and Quintana, with whom he developed the closest ties).

Perhaps it was the spiritual and moral support of these friends that maintained Cienfuegos's faith in the principles he had learned in Salamanca. His experiences after leaving Salamanca disappointed him, and, realizing the impossibility of all men adhering to these principles, he came to the sad realization that "insensitive self-interest" (P, 129) dominated and corrupted society. He observed the unjust treatment committed by selfish men who suffocate innocence and pleasure. In "Memory of My Youth" he compares life, in a brutal violent image, to the actions of a shipwrecked man who saves his own life at the cost of another in a stormy sea swollen by the hurricane of human passions. In such a world there is no place for the virtuous man, and Cienfuegos sees no other solution than to flee from his fellowman. This contemplation of the lot of the virtuous man is not the attitude of a man of the Enlightenment— the optimistic reformer—but rather it reveals a certain nostalgia and pessimism. But Cienfuegos never lost completely his faith in the ability of man to create a perfect, peaceful society. The contrast between the virtuous man's love for his fellowmen and the self-interest of many in society is a motif of Cienfuegos's major poems. Here, however, his pessimism predominates:

> Oh Batilo! Oh sorrow! Is it an indispensable law
> that to love virtue, one must hate man
> and flee from him as if he were a barbarous murderer?
> Oh painful truth! . . .
>
> (P, 130)

A good man, however, finds comfort in his own virtue and the companionship of a few friends: "his little-known integrity and a friend, / solitary like him, are his universe" (P, 130). Cienfuegos ends the poem with the recollection of the great pleasure he derived from the simple act of gathering, washing, and eating lettuce on the banks of the Tormes River. In expressing his praise of the simple country life, the artist shows his concern for the commonplace detail associated with nineteenth-century realism.

"Spring," another work with an important social theme, is written in twenty-three stanzas of twelve verses. All verses, except for the penultimate in each stanza which is heptasyllabic, are hendecasyllables. The combining of eleven- and seven-syllable verses can be traced back to the Renaissance. Neoclassical conventions of learned vocabulary and references to gods of the classical world blend well with the poem's serious reflection on nature, the virtuous man, and the poet's own life which, in contrast to spring, will never be fruitful and joyful. The first part of this poem is a detailed description of nature that differs from the idealistic vision of the anacreontic genre. Despite the classical and mythological references, the overall effect is far more realistic. The bucolic elements here do not contribute to that spirit of hedonism or escapism that characterized his early works. Nature serves to develop a more serious, albeit sentimental, theme than the pastoral hymns to Bacchus and Venus of the anacreontic genre, being not only beautiful and pleasing but also useful. Providentially, nature offers man whatever he needs. In his mature poetry, Cienfuegos portrays nature as a source of virtue and a solace to the man who suffers the injustices of society. The vision of a utilitarian nature, to which men should turn to rediscover their lost happiness and well-being, and a religious sense of nature are concepts common to poetry of the eighteenth century.

The poem, however, is not totally successful. There is considerable emotional license in the name of virtue and nature because the poet must have felt the bonds of society to be difficult indeed and, therefore, was carried away by his dreams of an ideal nature as a means to escape the onerous demands of civilized life. In his zeal to describe the grandeur of nature, Cienfuegos wrote some pretentious verses in which the elevated language fails to attain the level of his best poetry.

After the opening descriptive verses the poem glorifies Mother Nature, a refuge of pure feeling and love, as the motivating force behind the cosmic cycles. This depiction of life-producing love is juxtaposed to the contrasting condition of the poet, who considers himself blameless for his barren unloved situation. Like a romantic he feels estranged from society. He bemoans his fate, which seemingly contradicts all that he observes around him. The social commentaries that follow make the poem one of Cienfuegos's most outspoken criticisms of the injustices of society specifically the economic disparities: "The good man is condemned / to sweat and abuse / so that the evil man may swim in delights" (*P,* 107). Society does not function according to the basic principles of the Enlightenment: reason and virtue. The poet's ideal appears not to exist in the real world but merely in his dreams. He fantasizes on Switzerland as a utopian land where reason and virtue control men's actions and create a peaceful, happy society. This dream of a perfect society in distant Switzerland was probably inspired by the writings of the two major Swiss authors of the eighteenth century: Rousseau and Gessner.

> Fortunate country! Oh, how I wish
> I could fly to your mountain tops!
> . . . .
> Listen to a good man who,
> fleeing the cities as a protection from evil,
> seeks in this hilly harshness
> the peace and happiness
> which mother nature offers him.
>
> (*P,* 109)

In effect, the poet counsels man to retire from life to avoid falling into evil, which appears to be inevitable in society. Cienfuegos's poem reflects the ideology of the Enlightenment, which considered reason and nature to be united, since nature as intuited by reason was believed to be in essence the harmonious laws that govern the universe.

While Cienfuegos often spoke of his desire to flee the evils of society and to find solace in solitude, he did not mean to be taken literally. Perhaps he was merely conforming to a popular mode of the nature poets of the eighteenth century. Clearly, he chose not to live like a recluse, for he pursued an active social life in *tertulias* (circles of friends gathered to discuss topics of interest), as a member of the Royal Academy of the Language, and as an editor and government official. He apparently had a gregarious nature, as his many verses on friendship indicate. Poetic flight is brief, however, and the poet soon returns to reality. His meditation on spring terminates with the realization that his fantasies on the Alps will never come true and, unloved, "my spring will never be beautiful" (*P,* 110). The poem is neoclassical in its versification, mythological references, and elevated vocabulary. At the same time it is a very personal statement on the poet's own emotional state as well as a criticism of society in general. The momentary flight from reality to the utopian Switzerland of "Spring" is not typical of the writings of Cienfuegos. The men of the Age of Enlightenment were on the whole realists in that they were committed to improve the welfare of their fellowman through economic and educational reform. They were not dreamers desiring to escape reality but rather men who envisioned a better world for all men.

In "My solitary spring walk" nature plays an important role as the inspiration for the poet to meditate on the relationship between man and the laws of nature. The function of nature as a background for reminiscences and reflections on war and brotherhood recalls William Cowper's "Winter-morning Walk" and "Winter Walk at Noon."[26] The opening verses contrast the ways of life of the courtier to whom he addresses the poem and the first-person narrator. In the tradition of many poets since antiquity, the poet once more expresses the desire to flee the clamor of the city for the solitude of the country. That intense subjectivism characteristic of romantic poetry is evident in the poem: "now I see or feel / nothing except myself, nor can now / my mind brake the rapid race / of the imagination" (*P,* 117). The poetic persona laments his failure to find love, and upon observing the birds he envies their correspondence with the laws of nature:

> Oh, you winged lover, a thousand times happy,
> you are born, you love and in loving die!
> This is the law that, to be happy,
> mother nature dictated to all beings.
>
> (*P,* 118)

In contrast, man, contrary to a tenet of the Age of Enlightenment, fails to use his reason ("Nublada su razón" [*P,* 118]); instead he loves honor, gold, ambition, pleasure, and fame rather than his fellowman, thus breaking the chain of being:

> Instead of the love that unites men
> as brothers and equals, joining them
> with beings forever, he worships
> the unjust domination that breaks
> the union of the entire universe,
> and isolates man and the human species.
>
> (*P,* 118)

The poet preaches the need for universal brotherhood, a leitmotiv
in his poetry: "Blind Humans, / be happy, love; may the entire
world / be a beautiful dwelling of brotherhood" (*P,* 119). This
composition expresses the ideology of the Enlightenment in its
proclamation that reasonable men, loving one another according to
the laws of nature, will create a virtuous and harmonious society.
But on a pessimistic note the poem concludes that this hope is in
vain:

> . . . from the enchanted magic
> of my country of love I return to this earth
> of solitude, enmity and tears.
>
> (*P,* 120)

Unlike the romantics, however, his disillusionment is not total, for
he finds consolation in the love of his friends.

"To a friend who doubted my friendship" is written in hendecasyllables, as is typical of Cienfuegos's poetry with a serious theme.
These verses also typify the poetry of the Enlightenment in their
scientific-philosophical view of life. In this work the poet recognizes
himself as a part of the whole universe in which the basic principle
is the law of love. He meditates on the origin of an orderly nature
that developed from a primitive chaotic state when the sun, the
plants, and all of nature demonstrated love. Likewise, man formed
a civilized society through the power of love. Man became man
when he loved his fellowman. This idealized society had a pastoral
setting, and the poet found its origin in agriculture:

> Man obeyed, and the plow
> gave birth to society. There, man
> embraced man, for the first time
> all humanity felt in its heart
> all, all its essence, its entire soul,
> man was man.
>
> (*P,* 125)

This promotion of agriculture as the basis of brotherhood and the
perfect society may be related to the ideology of the eighteenth-
century physiocrats, who held that the source of wealth was nature
and, therefore, claimed the dominance of agriculture over industry.

It may also reflect governmental encouragement of the productive sectors of Spanish society as opposed to the nobility, who contributed little or nothing to the well-being of their fellow citizens. The creation of numerous economic societies reflects the epoch's concern for the welfare of the society through economic growth. Among the best-known examples of the concern for the industrious farmer as opposed to the idle citizens is Meléndez Valdés's poem "El filósofo en el campo." But this perfect society envisioned by Cienfuegos, where all men formed one harmonious loving family, degenerated, regressing toward its original state of chaos through a lack of love. Thus a principal objective of the poem is to demonstrate the beneficence of universal brotherhood, one of Cienfuegos's major themes and an important tenet of Enlightenment ideology.

"To a Friend on the Death of His Brother" contains some fiery invective against social injustice, greed, vice, and human evil. On considering death as a blessing, for it brings an end to suffering, Cienfuegos writes:

> . . . Ay! At least
> their eyes will not see the terrible scene
> of holy virtue tied triumphantly
> to the victorious chariot of evil.
> They will not listen to the obstreperous foot
> of injustice breaking the neck
> of unprotected solitary innocence;
> neither will they smell the sacrilegious incense
> that scandalous adulation burns
> on the bloody altars of power.
>
> (P, 139)

This attack against the evils of society is almost a cry to the oppressed to rebel against the rich and powerful.

Another social theme of Cienfuegos's poetry, related to his burning desire for universal brotherhood, is his antiwar stance. "A la paz entre España y Francia en 1795" (To the peace between Spain and France in 1795) comprises a fiery diatribe against war by a devoted pacifist:

> Where is humanity, the divine gift
> that nature imprinted on our souls
> at birth? May the inhumane man perish

> who first exercised the fierce ministry
> of murder! May the depths of hell
> swallow even the name of the evil bloody
> man who raised altars to valor,
> and girding his head
> with the eternal laurel
> said: may unholy cruelty be a virtue!
>
> (P, 100)

Written in 1795 to celebrate the Treaty of Basel, for which Godoy received the title "Prince of Peace," these verses recall the political poems of Quintana in their similar rhetorical effects. The elevated language, the numerous exclamations and interrogations, and the repeated use of imperatives serve to create the effect of a public exhortation to the poet's fellow citizens, symbolized by shepherds, an admonition to return from war to the peaceful solitude of their native mountains. The principal themes of brotherhood and peace reflect the spirit of the Enlightenment and like James Thomson, the eighteenth-century English nature poet, Cienfuegos "mingles the triple elements of conventional, real and cosmopolitan land-scape" in this poetic harangue against war. [27]

In "La rosa del desierto" (The desert rose), Cienfuegos employs the desert as a symbol of the barren arid world to which mankind, through its own fault, is condemned. [28] The rose in the wasteland appears "like sacred virtue / surrounded by a world of evils" (P, 150). The rose has the power to move the hearts and minds of mankind, and the poet thus contemplates the effect that the beautiful flower might have on some unhappy lost soul:

> On arriving where I am he will see this rose,
> look at it, sit beside it,
> and not knowing why, his heart wounded
> by a sweet tenderness,
> he will love, stimulated by my flower,
> moral beauty in its beauty.
>
> (P, 151–52)

The moralistic didactic tone of eighteenth-century neoclassicism is maintained as he commands the rose to remain on its rosebush to serve as a "school of love and virtues" (P, 152). "The Desert Rose," written in verses of seven and eleven syllables, reveals its eighteenth-century origin also in its intensely emotional tone. The selection of words such as "tender," "weeping," "crying", and "sweet tenderness" typifies much of Spanish literature written during the last part of the eighteenth century, for this period was also an Age of Sensibility. Indeed, Cienfuegos sounds much like a romantic poet when, on contemplating the flower, he takes joy ("un dulce encanto") in his tears:

> . . . I don't know what I feel
> within me, as deeply moved
> I give free rein to my tears
> and I find in my affliction a sweet enchantment.
>
> (P, 149)

Another poem, like "The Desert Rose," in which Cienfuegos laments the errors of mankind, is the elegiac epistle "The Graveyard School," wherein Cienfuegos, maintaining an appropriately solemn tone throughout, depicts the funeral scene in realistic familiar terms. After a graphic description of the suffering involved in the spectacle of death, there follows a thorough development of the ancient theme of *ubi sunt* in a solemn rhetorical style replete with references to figures and locales of the ancient world. Among the numerous classical references, the historical figure of Alexander is developed most completely as a symbol of human vanity and as an example of that ambition which causes man to be unsatisfied, living from one illusion to another only to find "anxiety and grief where he expected happiness" (P, 172). The moralistic tone recalls the teachings of the church, as does a reference to prudence, one of the cardinal virtues, but there is a noteworthy absence of Christian allusions or symbols. Cienfuegos and other humanists of the Enlightenment tended to divorce themselves from the traditional church, seeking to persuade man to accept the dictates of reason through argument, precept, and example.

The best example of Cienfuegos's moral and social poetry is the well-known "In Praise of a Carpenter Named Alfonso,"[29] a polemical hymn to virtue as personified in the figure of a humble artisan. Justice and reason, so admired in the Age of Enlightenment, are to be found among the humble of the earth ever since "subjugating man, / the first tyrant triumphed over equality" (P, 161). Thus from the beginning the poem expresses the ideas of equality, virtue, and reason, fundamental themes of the Enlightenment. In his violent denunciation of those powerful magnates who subjugate their fellowmen, he alludes to Tiberius, a symbol of cruel despotic use of power. Such allusions were more meaningful to the poet's contemporaries than they are to the twentieth-century reader whose education differs radically from that of the earlier epoch. The specificity of these allusions provided neoclassical poetry with a vividness and force difficult for the modern reader to appreciate.

Cienfuegos defends his innovative decision to sing this ode in honor of a humble worker, condemning those who call this upright man "ignoble and low" (*P*, 161). The form chosen breaks with the tradition in which the ode had been a genre used to sing the glories of the powerful (Cienfuegos once wrote an ode in praise of Napoleon that he later requested his friends to delete from future editions of his poetry when the French invaded Spain). Instead of celebrating the power of the crown and military arms, he sings the praises of the chisel and gouge—the simple tools of the carpenter's daily labors. Elevation of these mundane tools as symbols of the artisan's labors, incorporating them into his poetic vocabulary, indicates the innovative quality of Cienfuegos's poetry. The concern for everyday instruments of an ordinary laborer lends a realistic note to the poem, which otherwise conforms to the neoclassical pattern in its elevated language, learned allusions, oratorical style, and stanzas of seven- and eleven-syllable verses.

Cienfuegos defends the dignity of the workingman as an equal to all other men, a departure from class distinctions that was radical for the time. He seems to promote a hierarchy according to one's contribution to society, and scorns the nobleman who says to the poor man,

> . . . I am greater; heaven
> created you to labor; you in poverty,
> I in richness and power,
> your destiny is to serve, mine to command.
> (*P*, 161)

The diatribe against the powerful poses the rhetorical question:

> Can sceptre, knighthood, bloody sword,
> vile insignias of unholy oppression,

> honor the Apollonian song?
>
> (*P*, 162)

Clearly Cienfuegos's voice was a revolutionary call against the no-bility.[30] In contrast to the inactive nobleman is the virtuous hard-working carpenter who does not seek worldly power but is satisfied with his humble existence. The melodramatic and simplistic por-trayal of the contrast between the rich man, who embodies evil, and the poor man, who is a symbol of good, could have been justified by the state of Spanish society in 1798.[31] Cienfuegos virtually deifies the humble carpenter. The allusions to the "divine workshop," "sacred poverty," "holy Olympus," the trembling of "hell," and "angels" who call out Alfonso's name evoke the context of a religious experience that becomes most specific in the following verses:

> a common Carpenter: he embodies
> an inestimable treasure;
> he is the image of God, God on earth.
>
> (*P*, 164)

It is not without purpose that Cienfuegos chose a carpenter to symbolize the virtuous workingman. Cienfuegos need not have writ-ten the final verse above, as it only makes more obvious the already clear image of Alfonso as a Christ figure. Disillusioned with the lack of justice in this world, he finds the reward for virtue in heaven. Uniting the concept of virtue to the concept of immortality as an eternal reward reserved for the just perhaps reflects the influence of Rousseau's *Emile,* which also offers the idea of an eternal reward for the just man who suffers in this world.[32] These verses made this radical poem more acceptable. At least the author could not be accused of atheism. He also softens the radical or revolutionary tone by having the carpenter remain satisfied with his humble place in society rather than seek worldly power. This could be interpreted as a plea against actions comparable to what had occurred in France in 1789. Nevertheless, the poem remains a remarkable document of revolutionary political thought. "In Praise of a Carpenter Named Alfonso" is an extremely important work in the corpus of Cienfuegos because it best reveals how deeply ingrained in his personality were the principles of the Enlightenment. Here, in this ode to a carpenter, Cienfuegos demonstrates how far he had developed his belief in liberty, brotherhood, humanitarianism, and virtue which he had learned as a young man at the University of Salamanca. He believed that through reason and an acceptance of the laws of nature man could achieve a just society. But he observed around him ignorance and evil caused by man's egotism, and in this work he finds justice only in the next world. Elsewhere his dreams of a just, harmonious society are momentary before again recognizing that, in the real world, evil appears to rule.

Cienfuegos, in his social poetry, demonstrates the characteristics of those enlightened Spaniards who were able to combine a love for their country with a desire for social reforms, especially the elimination of intolerance and injustice through the brotherhood of men. There is no question that Cienfuegos is a didactic poet. The commitment to teaching his fellowman to be virtuous, just, and tolerant with the ultimate goal of creating a better society is wholly within the tradition of the neoclassical poetry written during the Age of Enlightenment. These poems evince a poet who believed his task to be the ennoblement of the heart and mind of each individual and even the elevation of the race to true humanity. Probably the most important fact to be drawn from Cienfuegos's verses is his deep commitment to the reforms necessary to create a better, more just, and more humane society.

The personality of this social poet committed to the spirit of humanitarianism closely resembles that of the *hombre de bien:* the ideal man of the eighteenth century as created by Cadalso in his *Cartas Marruecas* (Moroccan letters). In fact, in "Spring" the poet uses that phrase "un hombre de bien" (*P,* 109) to describe himself. Elsewhere, on describing a friend his verses indicate the specific private and public qualities of the eighteenth-century ideal citizen. These verses recall the epitaph of a good man that appears in letter 28 of Cadalso's *Cartas Marruecas:* "Here lies Ben-Beley, who was a good son, good father, good husband, good friend, good citizen." Although he never married and regretted deeply his failure to attain a lasting love, Cienfuegos obviously admired the qualities of an "hombre de bien." He too was a good citizen, worthy of the name "hombre de bien."

The vogue of philosophical poetry during the epoch in which Cienfuegos lived can be attributed to the increased attention given to discussion and analysis among intellectuals as shown by the popularity of literary and scientific *tertulias.* Likewise, the growth of economic societies attests to a more rational approach to the problems of the nations, while the general desire for improving society increased interest in moral and political themes. In addition, Spanish poets were obviously affected by the example of foreign authors. And, as always, there was a certain pleasure in being innovative by breaking away from the familiar love sonnets and pastoral songs to employ verse for a more rational, philosophical purpose.

Among Cienfuegos's more successful poems of a moralistic or philosophical nature, "The Graveyard School," with its unusual and beautiful imagery, vividly depicts death and its emotional effect upon a friend. Equally successful is "To a Friend on the Death of His Brother," a poem written to console a friend and expressing great affection and tenderness. At times, however, Cienfuegos's attempt to treat a sublime and serious subject fails because his language and rhetorical devices (repetition, exclamations, or interrogations) create an affectation that diminishes the poem's sincerity.

Language

The analysis of his poetic language bears witness to the culture of the Age of Enlightenment. Cienfuegos was cosmopolitan in his tastes, as his address to the Royal Academy of the Language attests.[33] In this discourse he attacks the narrow patriotism that opposes the introduction of foreign words into the language. Clearly Cienfuegos places himself among those who defended the modern spirit and disagreed with those who would blindly follow standards established centuries earlier. Cienfuegos had greater affection for the modern over the ancient, for freedom over rules, for linguistic cosmopolitanism over nationalistic purity of language. This spirit of innovation with regard to language and syntax is not surprising in a man committed to social and political reforms. Mariano José de Larra, writing during the height of the romantic era, comments on Cienfuegos's innovative use of language. He observes that the Spanish language

had not grown with the years and with the progress that it was to represent; this language that was so rich formerly had become poor for the new demands placed upon it; in a word, this dress was too tight for the one who had to put it on. Perhaps this may be one of the obstacles that our literary figures then had in order to enter further into the spirit of the century. One proof of this would be the accusation that has been made

against Cienfuegos that he gave the language little respect. It seems to
me he gave it a lot, considering Cienfuegos was the first philosphical poet
that we had, the first who had had to struggle with his instrument and
who broke it a thousand times in moments of anger and impotence.[34]

Heir of essentially sensualist poetics in the tradition of Meléndez
Valdés, Cienfuegos obviously sought in both his poetry and prose
to touch the sentiments of his audience. Thus his style at times
appears affected and unnaturally sentimental, as the nineteenth-
century critic José Gómez Hermosilla pointed out in his study of
Cienfuegos's poetry.[35] Hermosilla's criticism of Cienfuegos's choice
of vocabulary and use of imagery is similar to Ignacio de Luzán's
criticism of Góngora that appeared almost a century earlier. He
condemns Cienfuegos and his followers for having "formed an ob-
scure and barbarous language, composed of archaic words, gallicisms
and ridiculous neologisms."[36] José Gómez Hermosilla in his detailed
analysis provides numerous examples of Cienfuegos's unusual lexical
and syntactical usages that in fact demonstrate Cienfuegos's obvious
desire to create a unique style.

Cienfuegos did not like classifications by genre (the 1798 collection of his poetry has no grouping by genre) and the strictness of
literary canon, preferring open discursive forms to the closed and
favoring the variable cadence of the hendecasyllabic free verse both
in his major lyrical compositions and in his tragedies. Intolerant of
pedantic regulations, he did not seek a language conforming to
academic standards; on the contrary, he attempted to innovate,
searching for new and more intense effects. Among the neologisms
that he created are the participle "oreantes" (P, 75) from the verb
orear (to cool, to refresh); "electrizado" (P, 126), "electrified," the
imperative "desoid" (P, 161) with the meaning "do not listen to,"
and "rustiquecido" (P, 109) to indicate a state of being rustic. These
forms horrified the nineteenth-century critic Hermosilla. Cienfuegos
also made use of syntactical neologisms such as his common trans-
ference of the adjectival value to a substantive one and vice versa;
for example, "Soledades selvosas" ("woody solitudes") (P, 79) where
the standard expression would be "selvas solitarias" ("solitary woods").
Of a similar nature are the expressions "umbrosos frescores" ("shad-
owy freshnesses") (P, 104) to depict fresh shadows; "nevosa altivez"
("snowy haughtiness") (P, 104) to describe the heights covered by

snow; and "musgoso verdor" ("mossy greenness") (*P*, 105) to describe green moss.

Syntactical innovations include "ríe mil fragantes esencias" ("laughs a thousand fragrant essences") (*P*, 60) in which the intransitive verb *reir* is used as if it were transitive. Another example of an intransitive verb that Cienfuegos employs transitively is "pasear" (*P*, 65). Hermosilla objects to it not only on grammatical grounds but also as a gallicism.[37] Another gallicism occurs in the use of the verb *poder* as in "pueda . . . merecer" (*P*, 115) in the sense of "would that I merited it." The usage of this verb functioning in the optative mood is common in his poetry. Other gallicisms according to Hermosilla are the expressions "¡La alevosa!" and "¡la pérfida!" (*P*, 87).[38] Among the innovative uses of language is Cienfuegos's creation of the compound word "honditronante" ("deep thundering") (*P*, 99). He also employs "funeral" (*P*, 87) in the sense of "sad" or "lamentable." Another unusual lexical item appears in "La despedida": "me encerraré en el llanto" ("I will lock myself up in weeping"). Hermosilla complains that the verb "encerrarse" necessarily suggests the idea of putting oneself in a room and, therefore, is not appropriate in this context.[39] At times he used highly unusual metaphors, for example, "the woods of Minerva" to mean olive groves; "the tree of peace" to mean "the olive tree" and "to irrigate the ground with rivers of gold" for covering it with olives. (All three examples are from *P*, 113.) Hermosilla also complained of the synedoche "mimbre" ("osier") (*P*, 112) to represent a basket. The neoclassical critic did not accept new examples of metonymy and synedoche. But here again Cienfuegos demonstrates his desire to break the bonds of the past through innovative figurative language. The poet also was innovative in his description of the basket, using "vacante" to indicate that it was empty.

Cienfuegos occasionally employed words previously considered common or even vulgar and, therefore, unacceptable for poems of a serious nature. For example, in "The Shepherd's Walking Stick" he describes the protagonist's bald head, "su augusta calva" (*P*, 75). "In Praise of a Carpenter Named Alfonso" contains several references to the ordinary tools of the protagonist "formón," "gubia," and "escoplo" (*P*, 162). The introduction of such terms into a poem with a serious message demonstrated the poet's attempt to modernize poetic language. Similar common terms appear in the description of the carriage in "A Lover on the Departure of His Beloved."[40]

The word "sayón" (*P*, 99) is an example of a term considered improper in the context of the elevated tone of an ode. In sum, the language of Cienfuegos serves to intensify the emotional contact with the reader. His innovations, therefore, are related to the literary taste developed in Europe during the second half of the eighteenth century under the influence of the sensualist psychology and aesthetics. The need for a new poetic language arose as a result of the development of empiricism and an epistemology during the eighteenth century that provided a greater awareness of the importance of feeling and imagination. Cienfuegos perceived the necessity of a new language in order to give lyrical expression to these new insights of, and attitude toward, feeling. In the literary debates of the time the moderns objected to the inadequacy of classical mythology to express the new knowledge of man's nature developed by modern philosophers.[41] The continued spread of the sensualist philosophy caused such a reaction. Reason was no longer the single important faculty in control of man's fate, but must share its preeminent position with emotion.

Cienfuegos's individuality as expressed in his poetry provoked considerable negative criticism. Some critics may have been opposed for other than aesthetic reasons (Moratín and his circle of friends disagreed with the political thought of the more liberal group of artists led by Cienfuegos and Quintana). Others were dyed-in-the-wool neoclassicists who prized, like José Gómez Hermosilla, tradition over innovation, and therefore ridiculed Cienfuegos's verse, attacking the neologisms, gallicisms, and innovative syntactical construction. Antonio Alcalá Galiano, an acute observer of the literary scene, writing toward the middle of the nineteenth century, also reacted sharply to Cienfuegos's style: "The dialect he believed to be poetic doesn't go beyond being a senseless mixture of archaic phrases, words fallen into disuse, gallicisms, newly coined expressions and inappropriate, and unrelated epithets."[42] It is important to remember when reading such negative criticism that Cienfuegos was a philologist who wrote on the subject of language, a linguist, and a member of the Spanish Royal Academy of the Language. His innovations in poetic language must be considered, therefore, as a serious effort to reform literary style. This desire, unfortunately, was seen by some as antipatriotic because of the foreign influence on his vocabulary and syntax and because these critics believed that a poet should model his work upon that of certain Spanish poets of the past.

Conclusion

There is a significant difference between the poetry written after Cienfuegos's return to Madrid and that of his university days in Salamanca. While some later poems retain the elegance and polish of the earlier ones, whose most remarkable characteristics are the forms and themes drawn from the classical writers and their Spanish admirers, Cienfuegos's mature work reveals a desire to break away from a narrow interpretation of neoclassical tradition. The advance of empiricism and rational thought unquestionably had an effect upon the writings of the early neoclassicists, who tended to deprecate the importance of imagination in the creative process in favor of imitation of literary models. Another important characteristic of that group was their acceptance of the idea that poetry should present universal nature, avoiding the passions of the individual in order to imitate the sentiments of human beings throughout history. An important premise of the neoclassical aesthetic was that of decorum, that is, a certain elegance and good taste in the use of language, based on the tastes of a well-educated elite.

A spirit of freedom, however, was not foreign to the neoclassicists, who did not necessarily feel constrained by the accepted standards; they conceived the possibility of discovering new forms because they believed in the freedom of the individual to innovate within the bounds of good taste.[43] Thus, the mature poems tend to reveal a subjective view of the self and the universe with a concomitant innovation in language and form and a movement away from the artificial derivative world of the shepherd toward a more personal expression. The poet's goal in compositions such as "The Leave-taking" and many of his mature poems was to create as great an emotional impact upon the reader as possible through a vocabulary and imagery that did not follow the established patterns but effectively responded to a purely subjective view of the author's feelings.

Emotion is externalized via comparisons with nature, but the poems remain subjective because the first-person narrator reveals his own reactions to a personal experience. In other instances the relation of a personal experience such as a love affair remains totally subjective because there is no outward movement toward nature. Rather, the poet remains constantly egocentric so that he isolates himself from the external world, being preoccupied solely with an autobiographical description focusing on his private emotion. The advance of the sensualist philosophy during the century explains the intensity and directness with which Cienfuegos sometimes expresses his intimate feelings. Earlier in the century the neoclassicists, guided by the standards of decorum, good taste, and universality, refrained from projecting their individual personalities. Cienfuegos exemplifies an important development in the poetry of the late eighteenth century, that is, the employment of the first-person narrator to express feelings concerning personal experiences as well as events in society. Much of his mature poetry is characterized by the sensitive, emotional manner in which he writes about those events and experiences.

Chapter Four
Plays

The Eighteenth-Century Spanish Theater

During the late sixteenth and early seventeenth centuries Spain's dramatists produced one of the world's outstanding theaters, whose dramatists appealed to all classes of society, providing something for all kinds of people from the illiterate to those most appreciative of the baroque aesthetic. This theater did not rely upon any ancient critical texts; rather, it took its form primarily from the example of Spain's extraordinarily prolific master dramatist, Lope de Vega. Golden Age plays were composed in three acts, in a variety of verse forms with a shifting from one verse form to another in generally recognizable patterns. With these few exceptions, Golden Age playwrights enjoyed immense artistic freedom. The common themes were honor, faith, and patriotism, that is, an affirmation of the traditional values of Spain. They depicted the glories of the heroic past as well as the glories of the contemporary Spanish Empire ruled by the Hapsburgs. It was a theater of conformity with a remarkable absence of protest against the problems of society.

It is not surprising, perhaps, that in the eighteenth century, which saw a decline in the quality of dramatic productions, there would be a reaction against the Golden Age tradition. Thus, Ignacio de Luzán, who had studied the classical tradition in Italy, and others attempted to reform and improve Spanish theater by applying the dramatic theories of Aristotle, Horace, and their commentators.[1] Educated Spaniards felt the need to establish the neoclassical standards in their country because these norms had become the accepted practice throughout Europe. The level of a nation's culture or civilization was important to the intellectual elite, and the theater was an important means of measuring a nation's culture in the eighteenth century.

Luzán's *Poetics*, which first appeared in 1737 with a second posthumous edition in 1789, had considerable impact on the writers and critics of the century.[2] There was much discussion of neoclassical

ideas in the press, academies, and salons, and neoclassical theory
influenced Spanish literature well into the nineteenth century. Most
of the major writers of the middle and late eighteenth century
became involved in promoting the neoclassical movement through
critical writings, translations, or original dramas and poems.

The government supported the neoclassical reform movement in
various ways. Under Charles III, the staging of allegorical religious
plays, called *autos sacramentales,* and also of *comedias de santos* (dramas
of saints) was prohibited, in part because of their lack of conformity
to the rules, but also because some people were alarmed that un-
saintly actors and actresses were portraying the holy heroes and
heroines of these dramas. The count of Aranda, prime minister of
Spain, helped the neoclassic cause by establishing theaters in 1768
at the royal seats around Madrid and financing translations of regular
foreign plays to be staged at those new theaters. Major literary figures
of the time prepared the translations.

The neoclassicists' zeal to reform the Spanish theater led them to
criticize the work of the Golden Age playwrights. They recognized
the great talents of the earlier dramatists but regretted their lack
of restraint, manifested particularly in their disregard of the dramatic
unities and the distinction between the tragic and comic genres.
Lope de Vega and other playwrights of the Golden Age had blended
comic scenes with tragic action in a fashion that recalls the tragedies
of Shakespeare. While often maintaining a single plot, they usually
had ignored the unities of time and place by having the action occur
over a long period of time and with constant changing of the setting,
even to the extent of moving the action from one continent to
another. In the comic genre, they had not produced comedies of
manners in the neoclassical sense with the purpose of correcting the
vices of mankind. The comedies of the Golden Age were "social
throughout," but their moral teaching dealt primarily with a defense
of the social order.[3]

Neoclassicism carefully distinguished between tragedy and comedy. Each genre has its function, its subject matter, and its proper
style. Tragedy, a more "elevated" genre, deals with the actions and
passions of men of high estate, and should purge the emotions,
providing a didactic example. In consonance with the important
subject and noble characters, tragedy was to be written in an elevated
style. Comedy, on the other hand, was to be written in a plain
style, to deal with the behavior of common men, and to criticize

and correct the vices of mankind. The two genres should not be mixed in a single play because comic elements in a tragedy and tragic elements in a comedy would destroy the proper effect of each genre. An important concern for the neoclassical dramatist was the verisimilitude of his play. In order to maintain the illusion of reality, the neoclassicists stressed the unities of place, time, and action. Startling changes of scene were thought to destroy the whole illusion of reality for the spectator, who remained sitting in the same theater. Or if the action took place over a long period of time, the audience would have difficulty accepting the imaginary world of the stage. It should be noted that the often maligned unities do achieve a tight dramatic structure, increasing the emotional impact of drama, particularly in tragedy.

The neoclassicists considered the social function of art to be important and, therefore, Luzán's poetics stresses the utilitarian aspect as well as the entertainment aspects of drama. The neoclassicists gave great importance to the didactic element of the theater, which they considered to be a school of manners. Luzán writes that princes can learn to moderate their ambition, their anger, and other passions through the presentation of princes who have fallen from the greatest happiness to extreme misery, whose punishment teaches them the inconstancy of human events and forewarns and strengthens them against the reverses of fortune. Besides this, the poet can and should paint in tragedy the customs and artifices of flattering and ambitious courtiers and their inconstant friendships and attentions, all of which can be an extremely profitable school for teaching people to know what the courtiers truly are and to make clear the duplicities of clever politics and of that monster called reasons of state.[4]

Luzán provides an intelligent interpretation of the unities and the didactic purpose of art. In fact, the neoclassicists were not as rigid in their theory and practice as their detractors have declared. Leandro Fernández de Moratín stated: "The precepts should instruct and direct talent, not sterilize it nor repress it."[5] This attitude contradicts neoclassicism's pedantic adversaries, whose narrow vision focused on the letter rather than the spirit of the movement, which they often opposed for ideological rather than literary motives.[6]

The most important of the "rules" was that of verisimilitude, that is, the capacity to create the illusion of reality. All others could be reduced to the single rule that was the "soul of drama."[7] This, of course, implies that all rules cannot be followed to the letter.

Thus it is not surprising that Leandro Moratín, the most distinguished comic dramatist of the era, wrote that in the observance of the precept of verisimilitude "is included that of all other rules that are subject to it, and in order not to break this precept it is useful and proper to trample over the others."[8] This statement is significant, for it not only indicates the importance of the illusion of reality on the stage but also makes clear that this outstanding creator of neoclassical comedies did not believe in adhering to the letter of each rule.

By the end of the eighteenth century, when Cienfuegos was writing his tragedies, the genre of the "High Tragedy . . . was no longer purist."[9] According to McClelland, the dramatists of this period still respected the rules of neoclassicism, but "they no longer regarded the letter as more important than the spirit."[10] Dramatists began to deviate from the traditional idea of tragedy by introducing situations based on ordinary emotions and sentimentalized pathos from the popular eighteenth-century *comedia lacrimosa* (tearful comedy) or *drame* (drama). Cienfuegos's tragedies represent this change in focus with the blending of the sensibility and even pathos of other dramatic forms with a play that is essentially neoclassical in its adherence to rules. He and other dramatists presented themes of peace, happiness, and other benefits that they perceived as practical effects of the ideals of the Enlightenment.[11] Jorge Campos, on describing the theater of the final years of the eighteenth century, indicates the playwrights' predilection for virtuous, enlightened monarchs to serve as dramatic heroes.[12] At times there are attacks against despotism, but more commonly the emphasis is upon goodness and the sentiment of justice playing an essential role in themes of social inequality. Institutions are not attacked, rather playwrights blame wicked and ignorant men for failing to advance along an enlightened path toward progress and human happiness.[13]

The period in which Nicasio Alvarez de Cienfuegos wrote his dramas was rare indeed in the history of the Spanish theater. An epoch, for the first time, carried the name of an actor and not that of a playwright. It was not the era of a Lope de Vega or of a Calderón de la Barca but of Isidoro Máiquez, whose dazzling talent overwhelmed the theatrical world of Spain.[14] His first role, albeit a minor one, in the theaters of Madrid dates from 1791. He attained the position of leading actor in the company performing in the *Sitios reales* (royal theaters) in 1797, and from that time until he fell seriously ill in November of 1818 he dominated the Spanish stage. As the fame of this actor increased, a change in the art of dramaturgy was occurring. The sweet sensibility of the eighteenth-century tearful comedies gave way to dramas overflowing with intense emotion.[15] The triumph of Maíquez is linked to the success of these dramas. The ability to portray profound passions was considered the most important facet of an actor's performance, and in this Máiquez excelled. His great success was undoubtedly due in part to the unprofessional quality of the performances of other actors who destroyed the dramatic illusion in a variety of ways. There is no lack of texts that censure actors who chat in full view of the audience while a colleague is playing his role, interrupt their speeches to respond to the audience's applause, salute a friend in the audience, or listen to a soliloquy instead of pretending that they do not hear it. All of these obviated the highly prized neoclassical goal of verisimilitude. Máiquez, therefore, contributed to a more professional attitude and in so doing promoted a more realistic dramatic production.

Idomeneo

Idomeneo, the first of Cienfuegos's plays, had its premiere on 9 December 1792 at the Príncipe Theater and was printed in the second edition of his works, which appeared posthumously in 1816. He did not include the play in the first edition of 1798 probably for the same reason that the poem "In Praise of a Carpenter Named Alfonso" was omitted. Both have a radical, revolutionary message. *Idomeneo* is written in unrhymed hendecasyllabic verses and is Cienfuegos's only unrhymed play. The absence of musicality in the verses creates a serious, deliberate effect appropriate to the solemnity of this tragedy, which is a powerful story of love and death, virtue and deceit, reason and ignorance set in ancient Crete. The setting in antiquity and the plot taken from classical Greek literature provided Cienfuegos with a relatively safe, indirect vehicle to comment on the Spain of his time and promote the ideology of the Enlightenment. *Idomeneo's* plot is similar to that of Euripides' *Iphigenia in Aulide* and Racine's *Iphigénie*. Cienfuegos would have had an opportunity to see Racine's tragedy in Madrid at the Príncipe Theater in the month of July 1788.[16] Even though Voltaire's tragedy *Les lois de Minos* (The laws of Minos) apparently was never staged in

Spain, it too might have been an inspiration for Cienfuegos. Voltaire's work, like Cienfuegos's, is set in Crete where ancient, cruel laws, enforced by a superstitious and intolerant priestly caste, require that a maiden be sacrificed. The humane and enlightened king decides to save her and, after discovering that she is his lost daughter, overthrows the priests and the ancient system establishing the rule of justice. While there are obvious differences between the two plays, there are also similarities of setting, action, and theme.

Voltaire's *Mahomet* may have also inspired Cienfuegos to write *Idomeneo*. This tragedy is one of Voltaire's most powerful propaganda plays in which his deism is presented forcefully and the protagonist is an example of religious fanaticism, although like Idomeneo he is more "an ambitious scoundrel than a genuine fanatic."[17] This play resembles *Idomeneo* in that the unscrupulous protagonist gains influence over others through terror and fear, and his antagonist Zopire, like Linceo, opposes fanaticism with reason and propagates the concept of natural law.

Cienfuegos was obviously familiar with the story of Idomeneo as found in ancient mythology. This narrative is related succinctly in chapter 5 of François Fenelon's *Adventures of Telemachus*. José Simón Díaz reports that Cienfuegos proposed to Godoy that Fenelon's novel be translated from the French.[18] In addition, this mythological episode was dramatized by Crebillon père and by A.M. Lemierre.[19] It is clear, however, that Cienfuegos did not base his play in any servile fashion on any of these works, because he makes profound changes and gives a new meaning to the story of Idomeneo.

As the play opens the stage represents the Cretan city of Sidonia in ruins. To appease the forces of nature, the priest Sofronimo declares it necessary that King Idomeneo sacrifice his son Polimenes, explaining that the heavens are taking vengeance on the city because Idomeneo has not fulfilled the vow, taken when a storm at sea endangered his life, to sacrifice what he first saw upon his safe return to Crete. Unfortunately, fate determined that his own son was to be the sacrifice. Sofronimo's son Linceo disagrees, objecting that his father had formerly opposed the idea of making human sacrifices to an Olympus of vengeful gods. Sofronimo reveals that his purpose is to gain the throne for Linceo upon Idomeneo's death. Pretending to be divinely inspired, he prophesizes great misfortunes for the kingdom if the prince is not sacrificed. Idomeneo, tormented by the cruel dilemma, requests that the priest pray to God for an oracle. The opening act ends with the appearance of Queen Brisea, who accuses her husband of no longer loving her and is determined to discover the cause of his grief. The second act opens with a confrontation between Sofronimo and his son Linceo who seeks the man his father once was. Linceo attacks the abuse of religion by ambitious, hypocritical seekers of power and swears to save Polimenes' life or die in the attempt. Sofronimo reports to Idomeneo that the god of the temple demands the death of his son. In addition, Agenor describes a volcano eruption as a sign of the gods' anger. Therefore, the king decides to carry out the sacrifice. Linceo promises to save Polimenes by taking him from Crete in a Phoenician ship. After a debate with her husband on duty and love, the queen realizes the hopelessness of Polimenes' situation and commands her son to flee at once.

In the third and final act Polimenes and Linceo have been seized and are in the custody of soldiers. Idomeneo, adamant in obeying the will of the gods, orders his son to be taken away. The people, angered by the proposed sacrifice, attack the guards and destroy the altars and statues, demanding the death of the king and Sofronimo. Polimenes is wounded and Linceo killed in the ensuing struggle. Later, when Prince Polimenes dies, his grief-stricken mother commits suicide. Meanwhile the people have killed Sofronimo. Since he has caused so much tragedy, Idomeneo decides to leave Crete for some desolate land where he will spend the rest of his days. He names Licas, a member of the royal family, to be the next monarch with the hope that his life will be a lesson for the future ruler.

There are eight speaking roles in this tragedy. The five principal characters are King Idomeneo, Queen Brisea, Prince Polimenes, the priest Sofronimo, and his son Linceo. The three subordinate roles are Licas, Agenor, counselor to the king, and Merion, captain of the palace guard who appears briefly in the final act.

Idomeneo is loved by his subjects who see him as a "tender father" (1.1). The concept of a paternalistic, humanitarian king is a commonplace in Cienfuegos's theater. In his concern for the unfortunate, Idomeneo exemplifies the virtuous enlightened ruler whose major preoccupation is the commonweal:

> . . . Danger will never
> make me turn my back when
> the welfare of the public calls me.
>
> (1.6)

Idomeneo's wife complains that a once tender, loving husband returned from the battlefields of Troy a hard insensitive man. Brisea is not aware of the oath to the gods that ironically meant the sacrifice of their son Polimenes. Through this character Cienfuegos presents the conflict between love and duty common to his theater. Like Pítaco in the tragedy of the same name, Idomeneo longs for the pleasures of life in a humble hut, far from the false pomp of the throne that brings him anxiety and grief. Queen Brisea reveals his flaw when she accuses Sofronimo of forcing a horrible sacrifice from "a weak king" (2.6). This weakness explains his inability to resist the machinations of the priest, which result in the tragic denouement.

The hypocritical Sofronimo is one of the most distasteful characters of all Spanish theater. This priest of royal blood is driven by ambition and love to plot his son's ascension to the throne through the sacrificial death of Prince Polimenes. Sofrónimo has the opportunity to renounce the path of evil when his son confronts him with those lessons of virtue that Sofronimo himself had once taught and now contradicts (2.1). Instead, he manipulates Agenor, the credulous advisor to the king, and the king himself, threatening them with punishment by the gods, and even the complete destruction of the kingdom, which has already suffered greatly from natural disasters. He hypocritically invokes the "just heavens," "saintly piety" (1.5), and "mortal sin" ("sacrílego mortal") (1.6), and warns Agenor to "remember that the heavens are watching you" (1.5). Later he threatens the queen with the admonition "Fear the divine anger" (2.6).

After pretending to consult the god of the temple, Sofronimo presents to the king the dilemma of either losing his son or one hundred provinces, his honor, and the throne. Abuse of his priestly role to strike fear in hearts of others is his most striking characteristic. He gloats that even chance is working in his favor when a volcano erupts, and Agenor eagerly carries this sign of impending doom to the king. Sofronimo becomes so engrossed in his treachery that he rejects his son for whose benefit he is ostensibly acting. The epitome of evil, Sofronimo becomes progressively more isolated as the play reaches its tragic end, and in an act of poetic justice he suffers a cruel death at the hands of the angry populace.

Linceo is, despite his youth, a strong, mature individual with firm convictions and high standards of honesty and justice. From the outset, differences between him and his father reveal their growing estrangement. The debates between father and son express the different points of view concerning religious and ethical questions that were important to the eighteenth-century society. Linceo, who represents the ideals of the Enlightenment, which was opposed to the obscurantism and abuse of power as examplifed by Sofronimo, rejects the idea of blind obedience to what he perceives to be wrong. An outspoken defender of reason, he defiantly rejects barbarous rituals based on ignorance. His death exemplifies the tragedies that arise when reason is conquered by fear and ignorance.

Queen Brisea, a strong woman, defies both husband and priest in her defense of her son's life. When Sofronimo threatens heaven's anger, she responds that he should fear her anger if he dares to oppose her. She confronts the barbarous action of her husband by defending virtue and love as the source of law. For her, anything that contradicts her heart is not a law at all; she therefore represents the Enlightenment's concept of natural law. Polimenes, the ideal expiatory sacrifice, is noble, generous, and virtuous, the epitome of the humanitarian ruler concerned with the problems of the unfortunate. The sentimentalism of the period is evident in his tearful reaction to suffering and poverty. Polimenes is truly an innocent victim of fate. At no time does he reveal a flaw in his sterling character.

Agenor and Licas are minor characters whose roles are similar to that of the traditional confidant. Agenor is a credulous individual whom Sofronimo exploits, manipulating the weak counselor by appeals to his faith and threats of heavenly anger. He embodies the blind believer who through fear and guilt complies with the wishes of the priest. At one point he kneels before the priest and renounces his error, a scene with obvious similarity to an act of confession that exemplifies the play's fervid attack on the abuse of priestly power. Licas, a member of the royal family, is a contrast to Agenor and the spokesman for some basic attitudes of the Enlightenment. Like the Deists of the eighteenth century, Licas identifies God with nature. He reflects the spirit of the period in his sentiments of love and tenderness. He finds the idea of sacrificing the prince to be an unholy, abhorrent act and tells the king so. In this tragedy of exalted emotions, Licas exemplifies calm reason, advising the queen to control her blind fury. It is appropriate then that Idomeneo chose Licas to be the next monarch, for this virutous man will bring honor to the throne. The dramatist is obviously not attacking the institution of the monarchy as such but the individual unsuited to the office.

Idomeneo conforms to the classical standards such as the unities of time, place, and action. Unlike Cienfuegos's other tragedies, however, it contains no love episode. *Idomeneo* is Cienfuegos's first play and probably for that reason it contains flaws less evident in his later plays. He uses an imposing, pretentious vocabulary that he obviously considered most appropriate for a neoclassical tragedy set in antiquity. The occasional use of an unusual word order together with the learned vocabulary creates a somewhat difficult text. The elevated style of this tragedy is enhanced by references to Iphigenia, Agamemnon, Menalaus, and Minos—all figures from Greek mythology who have a clear relationship to the story of Idomeneo, who identifies with Agamemnon (3.9), calling him a great man for offering his daughter on the sacrificial altar while Brisea, like Agamemnon's wife, thought the famed leader and warrior a monster.

An effective, but perhaps pretentious technique that Cienfuegos employs in this tragedy is that of having the stage silent.[20] Act 3 opens with Brisea soliloquizing her distress over the fate of Polimenes after which she departs, leaving the stage silent for a moment. Two brief, silent scenes follow. In scene 2 Licas enters disturbed, hesitant, uncertain of what to do, and in scene 3 Agenor in great haste looks about with grave concern as if searching for someone. These two high-placed individuals depart in the direction of the royal tent. Scene 13 of act 3 is also silent. Polimenes has just been led away by the guards, and Agenor, uncertain whether to join Polimenes, finally stops deep in thought. In contrast to the silence on stage is the sudden uproar of the people who have gone to the temple where the sacrifice is to take place, an unexpected noisy interruption of strong emotional effect, reinforced two scenes later when Agenor describes the funereal silence that follows the clamor of the crowd. This sudden change from shouts or laments to silence also occurs in scenes 9 and 10 of this act. Silence in these scenes and elsewhere helps to create an atmosphere of fear and awe before the monstrous acts that are committed in this tragedy. Cienfuegos's use of silence as a symbol of death is most effective.

Ideological exchanges and debates, as previously mentioned, are another notable feature, conveying propaganda in favor of moral, political, and philosophical tenets of the Enlightenment. *Idomeneo* is likewise a powerful attack against certain religious institutions and practices. The extensive use of debates is a manifestation of the dramatist's tendency to lecture to the public through his characters. His overriding preoccupation with the play's message results in obvious lessons on ethics, religion, and politics when the dramatist would have been more successful artistically if he had opted for a hidden or indirect method.

During the Enlightenment the established church was criticized by some Spanish reformers who wished to eliminate superstition and to live by the principles of love, charity, and truth. However, Sarrailh reports that the masses followed their priests faithfully and remained indifferent to the attacks that this small group of men made against the church.[21] Cienfuegos's portrayal of the hypocritical, villainous Sofronimo is a violent attack against clergymen who exploited ignorance and superstition to manipulate their flocks through fear of divine punishment. Reason is defended as the antidote to the evils of blind obedience. Linceo deplores the ignorance that oppresses reason. For him the true oracle is not that of the priests or the temples but reason, which is "the only oracle that the Deity / gave to man . . ." (3.4). These two characters are the principal representatives of the differing points of view expressed in the play, with Linceo as the enlightened defender of reason and virtue who condemns the sacrificial rituals, lies, and frauds that are an insult to God. The struggle between generations can be interpreted as a conflict between the new ideology and attitudes of the Enlightenment and the defenders of the beliefs and practices of the past.

Among the religious practices that Cienfuegos appears to attack is the custom of praying to effigies, whether of God or the saints.

> . . . Deceitful men
> Speak to cold impotent statues
> Which treacherous self-interest has raised
> Upon superstition.
>
> (3.4).

Some men of the Enlightenment criticized the veneration of statues and relics of saints because of the danger of superstition in the practice.[22] Interest in the question of the proper worship of saints and icons thereof is substantiated by the fact that in 1787 a thesis at the University of Valladolid was written on the subject.[23]

Perhaps an even more controversial attack on religious ritual is
the obvious parody of the act of confession when the credulous
Agenor kneels before the priest and expresses sorrow for his error
in having objected to the priest's proposed sacrifice of the virtuous
Prince Polimenes. There is little doubt that Cienfuegos was sati-
rizing the great influence that the clergy can have over the credulous
and ignorant through the confessional and at the same time condemning the misuse of that power. These obvious attacks against
religious fanaticism and clerical influence over the conscience of the
faithful place Cienfuegos among the radical thinkers of Spain of his
time.

The eighteenth-century Deists often spoke of natural law—the
consciousness of right and wrong—considered to be a universal
principle that God engraved on men's hearts. This concept of a
natural law apart from the laws of men both lay and clerical is
expressed by Linceo, spokeman for the ideology of the Enlightenment:

> I call it unjust
> if it is opposed to natural justice.
> This is the supreme law, common and eternal,
> which it is not given to the Gods to change.
>
> (3.4)

These verses express a central principle of eighteenth-century Deism
which held that God had endowed the world with ethical laws that
every individual can discover, without the aid of authorities of
institutions, through the use of his own reason.

Natural law and natural religion were synonymous for many
eighteenth-century thinkers. Both assume the existence of a beneficent deity. Reduced to its essentials, natural religion consists of
worship of God and the practice of virtue. Therefore, Linceo sounds
like a believer in a natural religion when he deplores his father's
actions and asks, "What is virtue when the highest law / of mutual
love is broken in this way?" (3.4). The idea that Cienfuegos develops
here and in other works is that virtue is most essential for mankind
and that this quality of moral excellence is the product of reason
and love.

This tragedy also reflects eighteenth-century humanitarian philosophy. Preoccupation with the unfortunate of the world can be
found in numerous literary works of the period, such as the well-

known poem by Meléndez Valdés, "El filósofo en el campo" (The philosopher in the country). Both this poem and *Idomeneo* promote the obligation of the fortunate to assist the poor, expressing the idea that "one learns virtue / among the unfortunate" (1.4). Cienfuegos's message, evident throughout the tragedy, is that the primary goal of the ideal, enlightened monarch is the welfare of his subjects. In addition, the people's uprising against the monarch and his advisor reflects the spirit of an age in which the authority of the king was increasingly called into question.

Zoraida

Zoraida was first performed on 29 June 1798 at the Theater of the Caños in Madrid where it was favorably received.[24] It was also presented with great success in Madrid in the small private theater of the marchioness de Fuerte-Híjar, a lover of the arts and an adherent of the Enlightenment. *Zoraida* is generally considered second only to García de la Huerta's *Raquel* among Spanish tragedies of the neoclassical period.[25] The famous actor Isidoro Máiquez played the role of Almanzor when *Zoraida* was returned to the stage from 30 April to 2 May 1803. According to Cook, the receipts for these performances were satisfactory, but the tragedy was never performed again.[26] The theatrical manager and the company of actors may have decided to perform *Zoraida* at the end of April 1803 to take advantage of the publicity and interest in Cienfuegos that would have been generated by the opening of his tragedy *The Countess of Castile* on 23 April 1803.

Cienfuegos's dedication of *Zoraida* to Celima, a former lover, is of particular interest because it is an eloquent expression of his sentimental and melancholic nature.

When I recall my loves in order to give each one what my emotional nature owes to it, could I forget Celima, the lovable Celima, that Celima who made my heart the nest of her love? Time passed and our love flew away; but the nest remains and will only perish with my dying breath. Meanwhile, I take pleasure in your memory. . . . Yes, my adored Celima, I know that you cannot forget Cienfuegos, nor can Cienfuegos be ungrateful to the one who loved him so much. Ask my verses and they will tell you if it is possible for me to cease loving the one who has inspired entire works, the one from whose mouth I heard for the first time many of the passionate feelings that Zoraida later made her own. *Zoraida* is

yours; it wishes to be; it cannot help but be yours, it will consider itself
well rewarded if sometime you suspend your reading of it in order to shed
a tear, a single tear to the memory of Nicasio Alvarez de Cienfuegos.[27]

This dedication, full of tearful sentiment and melancholy, captures the mood of *Zoraida* and exemplifies the sensibility that appears
in many of the author's dramatic and poetic works. Cienfuegos
typifies the Enlightenment not only in his expression of passion and
melancholy, but also in his advocacy of its humanitarian ideology.
Zoraida blends perfectly these two facets of Spanish literature of the
turn of the century in its portrayal of the amorous and political
conflicts revolving around the tragic figures.

It is apparent that Cienfuegos wished to give his countrymen a
lesson on the contemporary political situation of Spain when he
chose to write this tragedy based on the discord within the sixteenth-
century Moorish kingdom of Granada. Historical facts are not reproduced faithfully. Beyond the hostility between the rival bands
of Zegries and Abencerrajes, the playwright freely modified history
to suit his artistic goals. This period clearly appealed to Cienfuegos
because it served him well in creating a drama to attack the inef-
fective, unjust reign of Carlos IV. Perhaps he perceived some similarities between the discord within Granada during its final days
as a Moorish kingdom and the turmoil within the Spanish government, which was soon to result in the downfall of the Bourbon
monarchy before the forces of Napoleon.

As Martin Hume reports, "Everything had been carefully prepared
by Napoleon. The Prince of Asturias had played into his hands and
was competing with the favorite for his support; María Luisa was
blinded to every consideration of maternal and wifely duty by her
love for Godoy; the poor, weak king, believing himself a genius,
was swayed to any side by his wife and her paramour; and the wily,
unscrupulous Corsican, with a fine army on Spanish soil, knew now
that he had them all at his mercy and could do with them as he
pleased. So completely had all parties in Spain been deceived, that
both Prince Fernando and Godoy, respectively, looked upon the
French bayonets as having been sent to support his particular cause
against the other."[28] While Napoleon's seizure of the Spanish crown
occurred a few years after *Zoraida* was written and, therefore, Cienfuegos could not have known that the inept reign of Carlos IV would
result in the loss of Spain to a foreign power, he appears to have

perceived in the discord a situation similar to that of the reign of Boabdil, the final Moorish ruler in Spain.

Cienfuegos played an important role in the promotion of the Moorish theme in the neoclassical period. In addition to his two tragedies, *The Countess of Castile* and *Zoraida*, he encouraged the translation from French of Jean-Pierre Claris de Florian's *Gonzalo de Cordoba or Granada Reconquered.*[29] Cienfuegos himself translated the intercalated poetry of the novel. The translation was dedicated to Cienfuegos by his friend Juan López de Peñalver.[30] Cienfuegos adopted from Florian's fiction a treacherous and bloody Boabdil and a virtuous pacific Muley Hacen, a friend of the Abencerrajes. Cienfuegos also used a law invented by Florian that demanded the death of the leader who lost the kingdom's standard in battle. In *Zoraida* and in Florian's novel, Boabdil takes advantage of this law to destroy his rival.

Another possible inspiration for *Zoraida* was *Las guerras civiles de Granada* (The civil wars of Granada) by Ginés Pérez de Hita.[31] This sixteenth-century historical work may have given Cienfuegos the idea of the Abencerraje mutiny in the final scene he uses to satisfy the need for poetic justice. This rebellion does not occur in Florian's novel but coincides with an incident in Pérez de Hita's history of the civil wars. Both Florian and Pérez de Hita present the love or supposed love between Abenamet and the wife of Boabdil as the cause of a slaughter of the Abencerrajes and a divine judgment. Carrasco Urgoiti concludes that it would be difficult to recognize *The Civil Wars of Granada* as a source for *Zoraida* "without taking into account the intermediate links that correspond to the development of the theme outside of Spain."[32]

Because the Enlightenment was an epoch of increased interest in scientific, historical, and literary scholarship the study and translation of documents pertaining to the period of the Moorish occupation of Spain were encouraged. Cienfuegos possibly had access to translations of Arabic documents. Among the leading scholars of Arabic documents was José Antonio Conde, whose translations, although not collected and published until 1820 and 1821, may have been available to Cienfuegos.

Zoraida opens with a meeting between Almanzor, leader of the Abencerrajes, and Hacen, the former king of Granada and father of the present ruler Boabdil. Almanzor and Hacen represent the two Moslem factions, Abencerrajes and Zegries, respectively. The discord between these rivals has brought great danger to the kingdom, threatened by the Christian King Ferdinand. Almanzor, just returned from Jaen where the Moors were defeated, accuses Boabdil of betraying and sending the Abencerraje troops to their death because the Abencerrajes alone opposed Hacen's granting the throne to his son. Boabdil's greatest anger is toward Almanzor's friend Abenamet, who was the most outspoken in opposition to Boabdil's accession to the throne. King Boabdil is also jealous because the beautiful Zoraida loves Abenamet and not him. Almanzor believes this anger and jealousy motivated Boabdil to give Abenamet the most dangerous role in the battle for Jaen, and now that the Moorish forces have lost their flag in the battle, the king can legally order Abenamet's death.

Hacen cannot accept these suspicions of Almanzor. The latter, however, reveals that Abderraman, the wounded chief of the Zegries, declared that the retreat, which left the Abencerrajes in grave danger, was ordered from above. Unfortunately, Abderraman died before disclosing all the facts of the disastrous battle for Jaen. The love triangle of Zoraida, Abenamet, and Boabdil is further complicated by the fact that Zoraida, without fortune and support upon her father's death, now owes everything to Boabdil and his parents. As the first act ends she begs Boabdil to honor his pledge to unite Abenamet and her in marriage. Boabdil falsely promises to carry out his word.

The second act opens with Zoraida lamenting the situation of Abenamet, whose fate depends on six elderly senators. The evil tyrant Boabdil increases the suffering of Zoraida by confronting her with the cruel dilemma of choosing between marrying him or seeing her beloved beheaded. She decides to be Boabdil's wife knowing that she will die of grief within a few days.

In the third act Almanzor encourages his friend to depart happily from Granada where tyranny reigns. Abenamet cannot tolerate the idea of abandoning Zoraida and becomes even more distraught upon learning that she has married Boabdil. Abenamet stabs himself with a dagger and, mortally wounded, hands it to Zoraida who declares that they will be united eternally in death before killing herself. In the final scene Almanzor and the Abencerrajes rebel against Boabdil, and the people demand Hacen's return to the throne. Hacen agrees to reign again and condemns his son to life imprisonment.

By maintaining the action in a single place and within the time span of a day *Zoraida* conforms to neoclassical principles, but with its complicated resolution, it does not achieve the unity of action. One conflict is the love triangle of Zoraida, her fiancé Abenamet, and King Boabdil; the other concerns the tyrannical rule of Boabdil and the enmity between his supporters, the Zegries, and the rival Abencerrajes. Although these two actions are constantly intertwined, the denouement of the play clearly demonstrates the dramatist's difficulty in resolving the two plots. The political question is resolved and poetic justice satisfied with the return of Hacen to the throne and the condemnation of Boabdil to life in prison.

The play conforms to the taste of the epoch with its numerous scenes of intense emotion arising from the love triangle. The sentimentalism of this drama is characteristic of Cienfuegos's theater and heralds the approach of romanticism. The tragic denouement uniting the lovers in death is a harbinger of romantic dramas such as *Los amantes de Teruel (The lovers of Teruel)* by Juan Eugenio Hartzenbusch. Also, the violent deaths of the lovers on stage would have been avoided by earlier neoclassicists, who preferred that the necessary blood or violent action occur offstage.

Zoraida, the heroine of love and political discord in the sixteenth-century Moorish kingdom of Granada, is not simply a one-dimensional character whose actions result from a single motive. This passionate woman's primary motive is her love for Abenamet, but she is also moved by Zulema's and Hacen's rational arguments to place patriotism and duty above her passion for Abenamet. Zoraida's lament against the helplessness of women in her society actually suggests underlying strength and willpower. Her expressed desire to be another Gonzalo Fernández de Córdoba (a famous contemporary known for his exploits in battle that gained him the epithet "the Great Captain") recalls Florian's novel *Gonzalo de Cordoba or Granada Reconquered*. When her confidante Zulema asks her for what purpose she wishes to be the Great Captain, Zoraida proclaims:

> I would challenge Boabdil, those old men,
> his council and my enemy, and however many
> traitors would dare to face my invincible strength.
> Fearlessly opposing their blows,
> I would either die at the side of my beloved,
> or I would raise him in glory to the throne.
>
> (2.1)

Zoraida also demonstrates moral strength by accepting the plea
of Hacen to love her country more than she loves Abenamet. Boabdil's cruel abuse of power drives Zoraida to despair, but, listening
to the wise advice of her friend and confidante Zulema, she again
accedes to reason and accepts her fate as Boabdil's wife, perceiving
her action as a patriotic service. Her capacity to respond to an appeal
to duty and patriotism in the midst of her tragic situation adds an
interesting dimension to her character. The presentation of this
dilemma and her decision to serve her country as Boabdil's wife is
not unnatural or unconvincing, nor is it merely a means of creating
a scene of intense emotion.

Boabdil is a tyrannical monarch whose misuse of absolute authority underscores the danger of allowing any ruler to have total
power. The eighteenth-century Spanish audience would have easily
grasped a message so applicable to their own epoch. Presented through
his own actions and the comments of others, Boabdil is cruel,
hypocritical, and selfish, in short, an evil man. Even Hacen admits
that his son is not as benign and virtuous as he might wish. After
betraying the Abencerrajes in battle and damaging Abenamet's reputation, Boabdil hypocritically pretends to be the latter's friend,
although he has every intention of destroying him. In his hatred
and jealousy of his rival, Boabdil becomes a monster. This symbol
of evil states that if he does not succeed in winning Zoraida's heart,
he will at least know how to bring fear into their hearts, sadistically
declaring that he finds pleasure in Zoraida's grief because it makes
her more beautiful. His punishments (life imprisonment and the
loss of Zoraida) are appropriate for a monarch who has so misused
his power, causing his subjects and his nation to suffer.

Hacen, the former king who avoided civil conflict and was a
father-figure to his subjects, considers the welfare of the country
above all, imploring Zoraida to love her country more than she loves
Abenamet for the sake of Granada. This wise, virtuous, and sensitive
man attempts to reason with his son and mediate between Almanzor
and Boabdil, the two impetuous leaders of the rival bands of Moors.
Hacen's attempt to convince Almanzor to restrain his desire to use
force becomes a lengthy debate on the power of reason to correct
evil and is a characteristic of Cienfuegos, who often employed a
confrontation in the form of a debate in order to present contemporary values or ideas.

In the final scene, Hacen asserts that his cruel son has harvested the fruit of his evil actions. The Abencerrajes led by Almanzor have mutinied, and Hacen pleads at the knees of Almanzor for Boabdil's life, offering his own in compensation. When the people demand that Hacen reign again, he accepts, punishing his own son for his transgressions. In this incident and certain other details, Cienfuegos did not adhere to the historical truth. But to comply with the neoclassical ideal of poetic justice, it obviously seemed appropriate that the virtuous King Hacen admonish his son with the hope that his imprisonment would be "an exemplary punishment and a school of virtue for him" (3.10).

Almanzor is the personification of true friendship. His anger and grief over Abenamet's misfortune cause him to take extreme measures to correct injustice. Loyal Almanzor offsets wise Hacen, the moderate Abenamet, and the more humane Zoraida. At the same time, there are obvious parallels with Boabdil, although the latter emerges as more villainous for using his power to cause the conflicts of the tragedy and ultimately the deaths of Abenamet and Zoraida. Almanzor stubbornly refuses to reason with his enemies despite the arguments of others. Understanding Boabdil better because he is more like him, Almanzor knows that neither law nor reason mean anything to a tyrant, yet Almanzor is not irrational, though his actions (such as his threat to take Boabdil's life) at times appear unrestrained.

Almanzor appears revolutionary in his refusal to accept the tyranny of Boabdil. For him the law becomes invalid if it serves a tyrant and not his people: "To comply with the law is tyranny, / If reason justifies noncompliance" (1.7). The suggestion that the solution to the misuse of absolute power is the overthrow of a tyrannical monarch must have been seen as extremely inflammatory by many monarchists and traditionalists, particularly in the political temper created by the French Revolution. The denouement in which Boabdil is removed from power and condemned to prison appears to justify the use of power against a tyrant. In the actions and words of Almanzor, Cienfuegos was undoubtedly expressing his political ideology and at the same time criticizing the government of Carlos IV.

Abenamet as a character is eclipsed by Almanzor. Fate appears to have involved him in the dual conflict of love and political power. In contrast to his friend Almanzor, Abenamet displays qualities of prudence, reason, and faith in his fellowman. Despite being of the enemy faction, he remains loyal to Boabdil through a sense of justice and honor. Under the threat of death he remains calm while awaiting the decision of the senators. He protests his innocence, but readily accepts whatever fate may bring him, not wanting anyone to think that he feared the law. In the final act, Abenamet becomes a passionate figure whom fate has destined to be born to suffer eternally. Confused, tormented, and unable to believe his beloved Zoraida, he resolves to take his life. Caught up in the web of a tyrant he can only escape through death.

The two remaining characters, the confidants Alatar and Zulema, enact roles essential to the development of the story, executing requests of the major characters and transmitting crucial information to the antagonists and the audience. Zulema has a greater role because she becomes directly involved in the development of the plot, persuading Zoraida to change her attitude toward Boabdil, to acknowledge her patriotic responsibility, and to make every effort to be a good wife. Zulema is not merely a servant but a dear friend, a source of reason and calm in a world that is crumbling about the distraught heroine. In his theater and his poetry, Cienfuegos made the theme of friendship one of his favorites, and it is fundamental to the action of *Zoraida* wherein Almanzor epitomizes the ideal friend who will go to any length to assist Abenamet. For the passionate leader of the Abencerrajes, friendship comes before everything, even his country. The ideal friendships of Zulema and Zoraida and of Almanzor and Abenamet function in the play as striking contrasts to Boabdil's hypocritical displays. Zulema's outstanding characteristic, apart from her friendship for Zoraida, is as a proponent of the efficacy of reason and moderation. Her role thus becomes more than that of the usual confidante. She resembles Hacen in her involvement in the development of the play's ideology.

Zoraida contains constant references to questions of law, justice, tyranny, and individual responsibility. The play is heavily laden with that ideology of the Enlightenment concerning the social compact. Cienfuegos's theater echoes the revolutionary ideas, as people kept abreast of events such as the French Revolution and the constitutional convention that followed.[33] The priest and respected literary critic Pedro Estala portrays the atmosphere of Madrid in a letter written in 1795 to his friend Juan Pablo Forner who was then in Seville, emphasizing that "Everyone has thrown himself headlong into politics. Everyone talks about the news, reforms, taxes, etc. . . . one only hears about battles, revolution, convention, national representation, liberty, equality. Even the whores ask you about Robespierre and Barrere, and it is necessary to have ready a bunch of fibs and gossip about the news in order to please the girl you are courting."[34] To appreciate *Zoraida* and many other works by Cienfuegos it is important to bear in mind that he wrote them in a society preoccupied with questions of law, justice, duty, government, and virtue—the very themes that appear in his writings.

The European thinkers of the eighteenth century were deeply concerned with the problem of reason and the passions. According to Lester Crocker, the consensus of opinion was "that men, despite their possession of reason, do not live like reasonable beings; instead of following their reason in some objective way, they prostitute it to their passions or interests."[35] *Zoraida* reflects this interest in the problem of the passions as opposed to virtue and to truth. Cienfuegos's constant references throughout his oeuvre to virtue as the ideal quality of the just man clearly implies that virtue consists of reason and will, which serve in overcoming the evils of the passions. This concept is clearly brought forth in the argument that Hacen and Zulema use to appeal to Almanzor and Zoraida, respectively. Abenamet's final words to his friend Almanzor include this important lesson of the tragedy: "be virtuous. / Virtue, Virtue; without it there is / No happiness on earth" (3.4). Man must control his passions because even if the object is praiseworthy, a passion may be harmful if not moderated. The goal of eighteenth-century thinkers was to create a better society through the subordination of the natural passions to a rational ideal, the love of mankind.[36] This lesson, obviously a basic tenet of Cienfuegos's thought, appears throughout his theater.

The Age of Enlightenment posited consistent progress in creating a more perfect society if man took a rational approach to solving his problems. In *Zoraida*, Zulema expresses this optimism based on man's reason and virtue. There was, however, an undercurrent of pessimism in the thought of the Enlightenment. *Zoraida* also illustrates this negative view of the nature of man and his institutions. In scene 4 of the opening act. Almanzor deplores the fact that evil reigns on earth and the virtuous man is in danger. Later Zoraida declares "That it is always virtue that is oppressed" (2.1). This attenuated pessimism explains the references to fate and destiny that abound in the tragedy.

The personal pessimism stemming from the unfortunate ill-fated love affair has its collective parallel in the pessimistic view of Granada's political system. The message that the political conflict provides the audience is related to a very basic question, that is, the liberty of the individual citizen in a monarchy. Power in the hands of a tyrant becomes the misuse of authority. In the denouement Hacen returns to power with the acclaim of the populace. The importance of the participation of all the citizens in government is also suggested earlier when Almanzor argued that the faith of the people as a whole in Abenamet was a better indication of his worth than the opinion of the six men constituting the royal council (1.6).

Ideology notwithstanding, *Zoraida* is a tragic love story, and for that reason Cienfuegos employed a variety of techniques to evoke an emotional response from the audience. It is justifiable to assume that Florian's novel influenced him to compose a play of such intense pathos. The passions, the lovers destined for a tragic end, and the effective use of light and darkness are reminiscent of a romantic drama, but the playwright's restraint does result in relatively realistic plot and characters. Cienfuegos does not resort to unexpected coincidences to move the action forward, but develops the conflicts and the characters in credible fashion. However, his failure to conclude the tragedy with the death of the lovers by appending a political solution weakens the dramatic impact of the denouement. Nevertheless, *Zoraida* justifiably has been ranked with Garcia de la Huerta's *Raquel* among the tragedies of the neoclassical era.

The Countess of Castile

The Countess of Castile was finished in 1798 but did not have its premiere until 1803.[37] In addition to performances on 23–25 April 1803, others were given in May and September of that same year and in May 1804.[38] Cienfuegos wrote a particularly sensitive dedication of *The Countess of Castile* to the marchioness of Fuerte-Híjar, a lover of poetry and the theater, whose salon was a focal point for artistic life. *Zoraida* was performed with great success in the small theater of her Madrid palace. Cienfuegos declares in the dedication that he views this tragedy as the best of his compositions. The dedication's repeated expressions of tenderness, friendship, and affection reveal the depths of sensibility of the dramatist—a sensibility also evident in *The Countess of Castile*.

The plot originates in a legendary episode of Spanish history. The events have been related in the *Crónica general* (General chronicle) and in ballads copied by Lorenzo de Sepúlveda and Juan de la Cueva.[39] The essence of the story is as follows: the mother of Count Sancho García, ruler of Castile upon the death of his father, falls in love with Almanzor, a Moor who aspires to the throne of Castile. To attain her goal of marriage and power she plans to poison her son. However, a servant discovers the plot and warns the count. Consequently, at a banquet Sancho refuses the drink his mother offers him, inviting her to take it instead. When she refuses, he forces her to drink the potion. In the eighteenth century, José Cadalso based his *Sancho García* on this episode of medieval Spain. Cadalso's neoclassical tragedy had its premiere in January 1774 at the Cruz Theater where it enjoyed a moderate success, but it was withdrawn from the boards after five days.[40] Also in the final two decades of the eighteenth century, *De donde tienen su origen los Monteros de Espinosa* (The origin of the Monteros de Espinosa), an anonymous play based on the same legend, was staged several times in Madrid.[41] The title of this play reiterates the tradition that the servant who saved the count was a member of the Montero de Espinosa family. In the nineteenth century, the romantic poet José Zorrilla wrote *Sancho García,* a tragedy based on the same historical legend.

In selecting a story from Spanish history, Cienfuegos was following a practice of Spanish neoclassical dramatists, who often found inspiration in the national history and legends. Nevertheless, he created a tragedy that expresses the sentiments and ideas of his own time by modifying the figure of the young Count Sancho García from a Castilian hero and innocent victim of the schemes of his mother and Almanzor, to a violent man who first rebelled against his father, later destroying his mother because he aspires to attain absolute power over Castile. The play reenacts the schooling of a young tyrant in the obligations of an enlightened ruler. The death of Sancho's mother is the crucial act that changes him into a reasonable, humane ruler. Cienfuegos also breaks with the traditional story by elevating the countess and especially the Moor Almanzor to heroic figures, motivated equally by their passion and the good of the people. Unlike Cadalso's creation, Cienfuegos's Almanzor is an idealized figure of the Enlightenment who would never consider asking the countess to poison her son. The virtues of Cienfuegos's Almanzor make the countess's love for him much more credible in *The Countess of Castile* than in Cadalso's tragedy. Another significant change from Cadalso's tragedy is the absence of chance in Cienfuegos's tragedy (the countess drinks the poison on her own volition and not by error). Unable to defy social convention, she sacrifices her life for the good of her country.

Cienfuegos gives a very different focus to the story than did Cadalso. As the change in title from *Sancho García* to *The Countess of Castile* indicates, it is now the drama of the countess, who has fallen in love with the man who killed her husband without her knowing Almanzor's true identity. Almanzor's passion for her is not tainted by any scheme for personal political benefits. As the plot develops, their love becomes united with their desire for peace and the welfare of their people. The countess is torn by two opposing motives—her love and her duty to the military policies of her son. In contrast to Cadalso's character, Cienfuegos's countess considers poisoning the count only because she is distraught by the incomprehensible cruelty of her son when he threatens to execute Almanzor and lock her up in a convent. The denouement's message of peace and eternal friendship between Sancho and Almanzor differs greatly from that of Cadalso's tragedy in which the two remain enemies. Obviously, Cienfuegos recast this legend of personal amibition to demonstrate the good that derives from placing reason over passion and public welfare above personal gain.

The setting of Cienfuegos's play is the palace of the count and countess of Castile in the city of Burgos. Muley and Almanzor (the latter hiding his identity under the name of Zaide) debate the peace arrangement with the Christians. Almanzor, a man of peace, seeks friendship with the enemy, whereas Muley fears they will be killed. Almanzor is confident that the countess, whose husband he killed in battle, will protect him (disguised as a Christian, he accompanied the count's body to Burgos, and there he and the widow fell in love). When he reveals his love, the countess confronts him with the dilemma of winning her favor by killing Almanzor. By the end of the act, she declares her love for this man, whom she knows only as Zaide, promising that she will have her son, who has already rebuffed the Moor's offer of friendship, sign the treaty.

The second act opens with a soliloquy by the countess in which she laments that she can neither love nor forget the Moor. Told that one of the Moorish emissaries is Almanzor, the countess orders him brought to the palace. The count, contrary to the established treatment of ambassadors, wishes to kill both Moors not knowing which killed his father. The countess, realizing that Zaide is Almanzor, offers to help him escape, but he refuses to flee. The act ends on a high emotional note when the countess seizes poison from Almanzor's hands and announces that she will tell her son that she loves the murderer of her husband.

The final act opens with Sancho overwhelmed by the knowledge of his mother's love for the Moor. In a reprehensible act, Sancho has divulged his mother's love for the enemy, and the news has spread throughout Burgos. In a highly emotional outburst, she rejects her son who rebelled against his father and now like a wild beast wishes to destroy her. In the concluding scenes, the despondent countess drinks from the goblet of poison that she had previously convinced Almanzor not to drink and now takes from the hands of Sancho, who is unaware that the glass contains poison. Before dying, the countess pleads with Almanzor and Sancho that her death serve as an example and that their friendship may bring peace to her people. In the final scene, Almanzor and Sancho kneel before her, each holding one of her hands in a sentimental tableau as they declare their eternal friendship.

The countess is extremely sensitive and even hysterical on occasion. She voices the anguish and loneliness of a sensitive woman whose characterization exemplifies the changing dramatic values of the epoch and the public's desire for dramas of great passion and even pathos. The countess's struggles with her emotions constitute the action of the play. She alternates between moments of strength and weakness, between feelings of duty and passion, between love for her son and uncontrolled anger. Some may consider the unrestrained display of emotions to be a dramatic defect, but it cannot be denied that she is, at the least, an interesting tragic figure.

The countess, like the heroine of *Zoraida,* offers an excellent role for an actress skilled in portraying a complex character of strong emotions. While she first feels compelled to avenge the death of her husband, she immediately recognizes Almanzor as the "Christian" who accompanied her husband's body to Burgos, and her love for him awakens. The fact that she fell suddenly in love with this stranger is not inconsistent with her personality. The epitome of the sensitive heroine, she bemoans "the sad gift of such a sensitive soul" (3.3). René Andioc considers the exaltation of her amorous passion for Almanzor to be expressed in verses that recall the heroine of García de la Huerta's *Raquel* more than they do the heroines of lesser dramatists.

Torn between her love and her sense of duty to her family and nation, the countess experiences great swings of emotion from love to hatred, from friendship to vengeance. Scene 9 of act 2, in which she pleads with Almanzor to escape and then tearfully declares that her love for him has brought her eternal grief, is one of many scenes of great passion in this tragedy. Similar exalted emotions occur in her reaction to the cruelty of her son, whose lack of compassion and understanding of his mother impels her to contemplate poisoning Sancho to "free the earth of a monster" (3.4). Nevertheless, the countess is a good person who has always desired to do what was virtuous. Consistent with Cienfuegos's other tragedies, there is always a conflict between good and evil public leaders, with the countess a representative of the type that Cienfuegos idealizes in his theater—the ruler whose principal concern is the welfare of the people. Her final words express hope for "Sweet peace for my beloved people!" (3.6).

As indicated earlier, Almanzor differs greatly from Cadalso's character in *Sancho Garcia,* representing calm, reasonableness, serenity, and restraint. Almanzor is a trustworthy spokesman for peace and friendship with the Castilians, whose goal is an alliance that will end the havoc and grief that war has brought to his people. He is a wise and just leader whose goal is the good of his people. His rational, prudent character is opposed throughout the play by Muley and by his Christian antagonist Don Sancho. Almanzor speaks like a man of the Enlightenment as he expresses his hope that "prudent reason" will bring compassion to Sancho's heart. Like the countess, he is a sensitive character given to sighs and tears, willing to die to satisfy her desires (1.7). In the tearful denouement, holding the hand of the woman he loves, he declares that only with his own death will be find a cure for his grief.

Cienfuegos's theater is replete with examples of perfect friendship. In *The Countess of Castile,* Almanzor exemplifies this eighteenth-century ideal. He does not hesitate to give his life to save Muley when the countess provides him with an opportunity to escape. As a virtuous man, his first concern is his friend's safety.

The young Count Sancho García, a rash tyrannical figure, symbolizes the evils of an absolute monarch with no concern for the welfare of his subjects. Sancho rejects Almanzor's offer of friendship and maintains a belligerent attitude until he witnesses the death of his mother. This arrogant, self-centered young man repeatedly demonstrates the potential to be an extraordinarily evil ruler who rejects all counsel. Sancho is jealous of his mother's authority, which derives primarily from the people's affection for her. Driven by his immense ambition for total power in Castile, he opposes his mother's love for the Moor and her wishes for peace. This obsession causes him to denigrate his mother by spreading the news of her love for Almanzor among the people of Burgos. He is unscrupulous in his use of authority, and shows no qualms in breaking the accepted rules of diplomacy that protect ambassadors like Almanzor and Muley. His boast that he and his soldiers are capable of conquering the world reveals his arrogance and lack of prudence. The portrayal of Sancho via his words and acts constitutes a criticism of the monarch who allows his emotions to rule over reason to the detriment of his people. He symbolizes the concept of despotism that the Enlightenment condemned. Sancho's hostility and scheming for power against his mother bears similarities to the relationship and activities between Spain's future Fernando VII and his father, King Carlos IV.

In the construction of this tragedy the character of Rodrigo is a contrast to the evil counselor Gonzalo. This elderly confidant of the count and countess consistently advocates those ideas associated with the eighteenth-century Enlightenment. Rodrigo does not hesitate to reprimand the ambitious count for his lack of restraint, appealing to him to reason before acting. The old man represents the liberal concept of the individual citizen's role in his declaration that a worthy man need not respect a king who allows his passions to carry him to excesses. As a counterpart to Almanzor, Rodrigo is the Christian spokesman for reason and peace, and thus his character gives a balance to the conflict of the Christian and Moslem nations. He is the perfect representative of eighteenth-century ideals in his defense of virtue.

Gonzalo and Muley have similar roles as confidants of Sancho and Almanzor, respectively. Both are chauvinistic, arrogant supporters of a militaristic policy. Gonzalo reinforces the count's opposition to a treaty with the Moors, while Muley attempts to refute the reasoning of the peace-loving Almanzor. Both use concepts such as honor, fame, and glory as reasons for opposing a peaceful alliance.

Gonzalo represents the evil that a ruler's counsel can commit when
he incites Sancho to usurp all authority from his mother, whom the
people love and respect, by suggesting that the count scheme to
destroy the people's opinion of her as a means of removing her voice
from the governmental councils.

Through these characterizations, which portray good and evil
among both nations, the dramatist increased the interest of the plot.
The division of characters echoes the conflict between reason and
emotion and the struggle between personal ambition and the welfare
of society. Characters dominated by emotion or fanaticism are indifferent to the public good. Characters whose outlook is reasonable
and prudent act to benefit the nation. In addition, the presentation
of positive and negative qualities among both peoples makes the
conflict more realistic than a play with only evil on one side and
good on the other.

The Countess of Castile contains themes that are characteristic of
Cienfuegos's theater. The theme of the heavy burdens of the throne
contrasted to the idyllic peace and solitude of a life far from the
court appears here (2.6). In the same scene, the corruption of courtly
politics is suggested in the countess's advice to her son. Furthermore,
eighteenth-century humanitarian philosophy permeates this tragedy. Love of one's fellowman is manifested by the glorification of
the virtuous person's desire for peace and the welfare of his fellowman. That this becomes the principal lesson of the play is evident
in the denouement's celebration of peace and peacemakers and, of
course, is allied to the tragic solution of the love intrigue. The
concept of friendship is closely allied to the theme of patriotism
which is prominent throughout the tragedy.

The Countess of Castile depicts the contrast between the chauvinistic, emotional patriotism of Muley and Sancho and the enlightened
love of country demonstrated by Almanzor and Rodrigo. These latter
characters represent eighteenth-century cosmopolitanism, which rel-
egated nationalism to a role secondary to the spirit of universal
brotherhood.

This lesson is closely related to Cienfuegos's concept of the enlightened ruler. The evils of a tyrant are manifested in the uncontrolled ambition of Don Sancho. His admission of guilt for the
tragic events of the play is a lesson for all in authority. Throughout
the play Sancho receives advice and warnings that would be edifying
not only for a monarch but for every citizen. Above all, a ruler

should permit reason to control his passions. He should not act on his opinion alone, but consult worthy counselors. He should always act in the interest of the nation and not for his personal glory.

The Countess of Castile, in its conformity to the unities, its elevated language, its characterizations, and the absence of comic scenes or other nontragic quality, complies with the standard conception of neoclassical tragedy. The unity of the love and political intrigue is particularly well conceived. It is not surprising that Cienfuegos considered it his best composition, although most critics would probably favor *Zoraida* among his tragedies.

Cienfuegos wrote *The Countess of Castile* in the *romance heroico* or hendecasyllabic ballad meter, a national verse form commonly used by neoclassical dramatists. The tragedy contains striking lyrical passages that convey the emotions of the passionate lovers and antagonists. An example of the imagery he employs occurs in act 1, scene 2, where Almanzor decries the futility of the enmity between Moslem and Christian with an extended metaphor depicting the contrast between the harvests of war and peace. The expected lofty style of a neoclassical tragedy is to be found in passages like the countess's patriotic response to the arrogant Muley in scene 6 of act 1. But the exaggerated, grandiloquent tone is limited in comparison to the earlier neoclassical tragedies of Montiano, Moratín, Cadalso, and others.

The Countess of Castile displays a noteworthy use of typically romantic adjectives such as sepulchral, pale, mournful, stormy, and sad. Another technique Cienfuegos used to capture the emotional tone of the action is the repetition of expressions, for example, "Abhor me, abhor me, I beseech you," "My son, my son, stop, stop," and "Oh, Rodrigo, Rodrigo, if you love him." Francisco Martínez de la Rosa, one of the leading authors of the first half of the nineteenth century, faults Cienfuegos for a lack of realism in the play.[43] Perhaps Martínez de la Rosa was justified in his complaint, but upon considering the contemporary theater and the tragedies of the approaching romantic movement with which *The Countess of Castile* bears similarities through the ill-fated love of the heroine and the pathos of the denouement, Cienfuegos's tragedy does not suffer from an excess of improbable incidents.

As in his other tragedies, Cienfuegos uses debates to convey opposing points of view and propound the contemporary ideology. His emphasis on the creation of episodes that result in emotionally charged confrontations is a striking technique of *The Countess of Castile*. Debates between Almanzor and Muley, Sancho and Rodrigo, the countess and Almanzor, and mother and son produce moments of immense passion and conflicts between strong emotions and prudent reason. These scenes culminate in the pathos of the final scene where Almanzor and Sancho kneel before the dying countess and declare eternal friendship and peace. The final silent tableau augments the emotional impact of the tragedy.

Pítaco

Pítaco apparently was never performed but did appear in the second edition of Cienfuegos's works published by the Royal Press in 1816. This tragedy was presented at a poetic contest suggested by Jovellanos and sponsored by the Royal Academy of the Language but did not win the prize. According to Marcelino Menéndez Pelayo, the Academy did not award Cienfuegos a prize for this play because they found it to be too revolutionary although, as a reward for his effort, they opened their doors to him.[44]

Pítaco is reminiscent of the *Electra* plays written by Euripides and Sophocles in that all involve the return of the son of an assassinated king who conspires to avenge the death of his father. The play opens with the arrival of Faon, son of the former king, and Alceo, his counselor and fellow exile, in the palace of Pítaco, king of Lesbos and one of the wise men of Greece. They have returned from exile to find that Faon's assassinated father has been replaced on the throne by Pítaco. The citizens demanded that Pítaco be king after the death of Melancro, the previous monarch, believing that his generous and good nature would put an end to the discord and unpunished criminal activity in the kingdom. Faon recognizes the sterling character of King Pítaco and declares that the new monarch was not an accomplice in the murder of his father. However, Alceo, companion and advisor to Faon, maliciously denigrates Pítaco, inciting Faon to destroy Pítaco and seize the throne. Alceo's lust for power knows no bounds. He sugggests that Faon marry Safo, King Pítaco's adopted daughter, in order to use her to overthrow Pítaco. Safo's passionate love for Faon is tested when he demands that she kill Pítaco. Despite the treachery of those whom he has treated generously, Pítaco stubbornly insists upon pardoning them. The conspirators Alceo and Faon, however, reject all offers of friendship and choose to wage war against the king. On being informed that his beloved daughter Safo accompanies the conspirators in battle, Pítaco momentarily experiences an abrupt change of personality and demands the death of the rebels, but reverts from this uncharacteristic spirit of vengeance when Safo returns repentant.

The victorious forces loyal to Pítaco report that Faon has escaped by ship and that they have captured the traitorous Alceo whom Pítaco now pardons. The play ends with the noble, exemplary king renouncing the throne for the simple country life far from the plots and rancors of the court because he has been unable to bring total harmony and happiness to his people. The final happy solution to his difficulties does not negate Pítaco's role as a tragic hero according to neoclassic theory, which permitted such benign denouements. What is essential is that the vicissitudes of a high-ranking character arouse terror and pity in the audience; of secondary importance is whether the final resolution is a happy or an unhappy one.

Cienfuegos achieves a certain neatness in the development of the action and the solution of the difficulties in which he placed his protagonist. Neoclassical theory provided sufficient reason for a simpler plot and scenic pattern than are commonly found in the baroque and romantic epochs. Application of the unities of time, place, and action prohibited episodes extraneous to the principal action; brought the antagonists in close proximity to one another; and focused on a brief moment in the lives of the characters, all of which tended to heighten the conflict by narrowing it to one setting, one plot line, and a limited period of time. The result of such a telescoping of the dramatist's view frequently produced, as in *Pítaco,* a drama of great emotional intensity.

Cienfuegos devised a plot that generated scenes to illustrate repeatedly the essential opposition between good and evil, generosity and selfishness, friendship and enmity. In giving such emphasis, however, the dramatist eliminated all psychological subtlety by reducing characterization to insignificance. Perhaps this emphasis on an orderly design of episodes to exemplify the theme arises from a belief that the essential quality of dramatic excellence resides in perfect ordering of the action. In this, he probably was complying with the first principle of Aristotle's *Poetics,* that plot is the soul of tragedy. A careful examination of the play, however, leads to a conviction that in the last analysis the action was a contrivance of secondary interest with Cienfuegos, who managed plot in such a way that it appears as though his goal was to produce as many confrontations as possible. Each episode serves to create a scene of intense emotions, indicating that the dramatist gave only secondary importance to the credibility of events and that his primary desideratum was the displaying of passions and sentiments. Thus the plot of *Pítaco* is less an orderly development of the story than a device for presenting outbursts of emotion and contrasting values.

Each episode produces a crisis that the dramatist treats so as to display intense states of passion, sharp clashes in point of view between two opposing characters, the consideration of conflicting possibilities of choice, or the persuasion of one character by another. Pítaco is repeatedly confronted with situations that offer him the opportunity to react with magnanimity when confronting his treacherous enemies. The magnanimous gesture of the hero forgiving his enemy exemplifies Pítaco's reaction to the sharp clashes of will or point of view that he constantly faces. Similarly, Cienfuegos creates situations for Safo to express intense emotion as she weighs conflicting possibilities of choice arising from her love for Faon and her love and sense of duty to the king who adopted and raised her. Scenes in which one character persuades another also display great tension, as in the relationship between Alceo and Faon, when the evil counselor with virulent sarcasm incites Faon to attempt to usurp the throne.

The plot is so contrived as frequently to place the characters, in particular Pítaco, in situations requiring an extreme manifestation of their virtues or failings, affording frequent occasion for passionate outbursts or laments. The result is that the characters, most obviously the hero, lack the psychological depth that is generally considered essential for superior characterization. Cienfuegos created a bigger-than-life protagonist and involved him in a sequence of episodes where he serves as a mouthpiece for elevated sentiments and strong passions.

The characters are limited to six, satisfying neoclassical norms, and these few roles are balanced between the forces of good and evil. Pítaco and Faon as king and prince represent opposing royal figures; Fanes and Alceo are counselors, respectively, to Pítaco and Faon; Tares commands the forces loyal to Pítaco against the rebels; while Safo, as Pítaco's adopted daughter and Faon's fiancée, can be considered as part of both camps.

The action and the characterizations are appropriate for a tragedy in that the intrigue revolves around a lofty personage who, because of the ambition and vengeance of others, ultimately suffers a great change in fortune when he abandons the crown in favor of a simple life far from the court. The king and other characters conform to the neoclassical standard of decorum in that their actions are appropriate for their position, age, sex, and dignity. They are also consistent, that is, they sustain the same character or disposition throughout the drama. Pítaco's renunciation of his power is an acceptable change in his characterization because it is sufficiently motivated and occurs at the end of the play.

Pítaco is the prototype of an enlightened king, generous toward both his enemies and his friends. His greatest virtue is his friendship for all men, because the only goal that he has is the happiness of his people and the tranquillity of his nation; his values are those of a humanitarian ruler. Many of the ruling class would not have accepted the idea that a king should abdicate because he has not achieved an ideal state in which all citizens are content. Cienfuegos's verses express a view contrary to the traditional concept that a monarch's right to rule comes from God, insinuating democratic humanitarian values and indirect attacks against the concept of absolute power, which may have caused the Royal Academy of the Language to consider the play to be too revolutionary.

The play is a typical example of the eighteenth-century literature of persuasion, as becomes obvious when the hero who "never knowingly offended anyone" declares in the final words of the drama, "And I will be overjoyed if my punishment / Can serve as an example for others!" (3.10). At the opposite extreme, Alceo is the epitome of the evil confidant and advisor, unable to control his hatred for Pítaco nor his lust for power, lying and deceiving in his futile attempt to overthrow the monarch. His cunning use of argument, sarcasm, and appeals to the memory of Faon's father convinces the latter to undertake the dangerous task of rebelling. In this drama of virtue and evil, Alceo and the overcredulous Faon stand in stark contrast to the enlightened King Pítaco.

Safo, one of the secondary characters, serves to complicate the intrigue, introducing the theme of sexual love as a contrast to the protagonist's humanitarian love. Her presence allows the dramatist to heighten the evil committed by Pítaco's antagonists, Alceo and Faon. Safo's betrayal of her father provides a means of giving the protagonist a touch of humanity, as he angrily vows vengeance for the treachery, while her departure and return motivate emotion-packed speeches.

The role of Fanes is that of the typical confidant whose dialogues with the protagonist allow the latter to express his inner feelings. Pítaco reveals to Fanes and thus to the audience his distaste for the throne that has caused him many tribulations. Also, the enlightened monarch expresses the humanitarian ideals of the epoch to his confidant, for example, that it is better "to die loving all mankind / than to live hating and fearing them" (1.7).

Tares, the trusted friend of King Pítaco and loyal commander of his forces, like the other characters is present on stage as a means of reinforcing the image of the hero as a humane and virtuous ruler. Alceo attempts in vain to destroy the bond of friendship between Tares and Pítaco. The king, true to his character, refuses to question the loyalty of his general, for he is unable to harbor the idea of treachery in a man whom he had held as a trusted friend. Upon hearing of the conspiracy to usurp the throne, Tares immediately declares his intention to punish their treachery, providing Pítaco an opportunity to express the message that mankind commits errors through blindness or ignorance and that man needs an example to teach him virtue, for only through the love of virtue will he behave uprightly (2.8).

In conformity with the Horatian and neoclassical requirement that a literary work be both entertaining and useful, Cienfuegos promulgates an important message that demonstrates the strong impact that the ideology of the Enlightenment had on the dramatist. Virtue, as depicted in the eighteenth-century ideal man (hombre de bien) is explained and described by Pítaco to General Tares who advocates severity and torture while decrying pity and compassion for the rebels (2.8). In his fiery argument against the use of force, the philosopher king implies that only the virtuous man attains true satisfaction or happiness and, therefore, his words are related to the eighteenth-century discussion on the relationship between virtue and happiness. Lester G. Crocker describes the debate thus:

The philosophies of hedonism or eudaemonism, and of social utilitarianism, sometimes held conjointly by the same men, constitute a dichotomy which the eighteenth century was compelled to resolve. If self-interest is the only motive and happiness the only goal of conduct, and if, simultaneously, the locus of value is placed outside the particular sentient individual, a reconciliation becomes urgent. Moreover, if virtue is defined in terms of happiness, and if it is assumed that there is no natural impulse or reason to prefer the interest of others to our own, the amoralist must perforce triumph, unless it can be shown that there is an indissoluble, invariable identity between the two terms, virtue and happiness. This was the central problem of ethics for eighteenth-century thinkers, one with which they were faced as a result of their analysis of human nature and their reduction of moral experience to reactions of pleasure and pain.[45]

According to Crocker, eighteenth-century philosophers (like the Greeks) "were not asking, 'What ought I to do?' but 'How should I live in order to achieve happiness?' "[46] Pítaco's rejection of society for the solitude of the simple natural life far from the court is the act of a man who has accepted his failure to persuade those who are not moral to be moral. Cienfuegos must have had the insight to understand, like Hume, that "moral skepticism cannot be countered by providing reasons to persuade those who are not moral to become moral. This is one of the reasons why the eighteenth-century enterprise was bound to fail."[47]

Pítaco deals with another important theme of the Enlightenment, the relationship between the monarch and the citizens of his domain. The idea of a just ruler is established in the opening scene and is reiterated, significantly, in the final scene when Pítaco acknowledges man's ambivalent posture before good and evil and again emphasizes the relationship between ruler and ruled. He is fully aware of the unjust ruler's potential for abusing his power and bringing suffering upon his subjects.

Another major theme, that of brotherhood, appears in Pítaco's constant references to "friendship" and "love." He generously welcomes Faon and Alceo on their return to his kingdom by restoring their possessions and placing at their disposal his personal wealth and power. Pítaco's unquestioning friendship is almost a mania setting him above ordinary men. Even the conspiracy of Alceo and Faon to dethrone him does not sway the king from maintaining his virtuous equanimity. Pítaco incarnates the centuries-old vision of the nobility of the simple man who lives apart from the corrupting forces of society. The people had demanded that Pítaco be their ruler and, therefore, he left his humble dwelling, returning to it at the end.

Neoclassical theory dictated that a tragedy portray the death or downfall of an important figure. The sudden decision of Pítaco to renounce the pomp and power of a monarch would constitute such a sudden reversal of fortune. His final speech in which he abandons the throne provides a lesson for other men in authority, a message of compassion, forgiveness, and justice. A salient aspect of this speech is the expression of a moral defeat. This idea also appears in the opening scenes of the final act where he mentions "barbarous desires" (3.1) and, frightened by his own anger, states, "Perhaps some day I will become a tyrant" (3.2). There is a tragic sense to his lament over the evils of the court, which has produced in him a "cruel sadness" and the fear that he may not be able to uphold his high moral standards (3.10). *Pítaco* also conforms to neoclassical norms for tragedy in its elevated language and treatment of lofty personages of high rank, as well as the great change of fortune in the life of the protagonist. Clearly, it differs radically from many eighteenth-century tragedies whose protagonists, ruled by their passions, violated their subjects and offended heaven, exciting terror and compassion in the hearts of the spectators through their bloody, violent denouements. Unlike Cienfuegos's other tragedies, the ending of *Pítaco* may be seen as a happy one even though it is also touchingly sad that the hero perceives an obligation to renounce the throne despite the people's desire that he continue to reign. But the hero is obviously pleased as he announces his decision to return to the rural setting of his childhood, a pleasant environment of natural simplicity and virtues totally opposed to the hypocrisy and corruption of the court. Obviously, the passions of pity and terror, considered proper to tragedy in the Aristotelian tradition, are not as important in this play as a feeling of admiration for the hero who never appears to be in real danger of losing his life. Cienfuegos has created a hero of godlike virtue whose love for all mankind and merciful pardoning of those who wrong him have a divine quality that evokes admiration rather than pity or terror.

Pítaco exemplifies Cienfuegos's didactic conception of tragedy, that is, that it be a school for virtue. The view that tragedy has a didactic moral purpose was, of course, a commonplace throughout the eighteenth century, and ethical sentiment is the moving force behind the world of *Pítaco*. The moral becomes the emotional embracing of virtue and rejection of evil, rather than the realization of divine providence. In *Pítaco,* the dramatist's primary concern appears to have been the evoking of emotion with a concomitant diminution in the importance of the plot in contrast to the traditional view of drama. Lessening the significance of the plot led to an emphasis on the parts or situations instead of the whole. Cienfuegos seemingly conceived the beauty of tragedy as inhering in passionate speeches rather than the intrigue of extraordinary events. If *Pítaco* be judged in light of this vision of tragedy, then the dramatist succeeded in creating a moving dramatic piece, for he achieved empathy for the characters through their moral dilemmas and stirred the emotions through their passionate discourses. These sentimental tragedies emphasizing a series of passionate, distressful situations typify a dramaturgy in which the play, to be persuasive and pleasurable, required sensationalism, a need apparently developed from the Aristotelian vision, which held that certain emotions associated with tragedy act as the agents of moral force.

Cienfuegos's Tragic Art

Cienfuegos's four tragedies have many features characteristic of the neoclassical theater. Three are written in eleven-syllable verse with assonant rhyme in the even-numbered lines, a form called *romance heroico,* the metrical form most commonly used in Spanish neoclassical tragedies. *Idomeneo* is the exception, and there he also employed the hendecasyllabic line but without rhyme. The lengthy eleven-syllable verses were favored because they produce a deliberate effect appropriate to tragedy. In addition, longer lines lessen the musicality of the dialogue by maintaining the vowel rhymes at a lengthy distance, thus contributing a serious tone suitable for the tragic action. The high quality of the poetry of these tragedies is not surprising because Cienfuegos is generally considered, as a poet, to surpass the other neoclassicists who attempted to renew the Spanish stage through the composition of "regular" tragedies. His dramatic poetry has a warmth and vitality generally lacking in other Spanish neoclassical tragedies.[48] In *Pítaco,* however, the grandiloquent, sublime, rhetorical language associated with the usual neoclassical effort predominates. The artificial quality of the dialogue in *Pítaco,* and to a lesser extent in Cienfuegos's remaining tragedies, is not necessarily to be judged a defect in the neoclassic theater, particularly in tragedy, which aspires to a stylized effect. The tendency of Cienfuegos to have his characters deliver formal speeches rather than converse more naturally creates an effect that the neoclassicists would not have questioned, but which the modern reader would consider artificial.

Cienfuegos consistently employed a three-act structure whereas standard neoclassical practice was to develop the action in five acts. The action of the tragedies progresses principally through dialogue. The exception to this technique (an important one) are the mute scenes that occur primarily in *Idomeneo*. These scenes, which leave an actor on stage in silence, permit the character to express thoughts and emotions through gestures and movements that advance the action of the tragedy.

Neoclassical theory favored subjects taken from the historical and legendary past. Cienfuegos made use of themes from both classical antiquity and medieval Spain in creating his tragedies. He was not alone in basing his tragedies on Spanish events, for many of the neoclassicists looked to the national history for inspiration. Through plots set in a distant past in both a temporal and spatial sense, Cienfuegos succeeded in demonstrating to his eighteenth-century audience the universality of the struggle between "reason and the passions, natural order and social disorder."[49] Common to all of Cienfuegos's theater is the creation of a struggle between love and duty. Much dramatic tension derives from this conflict, as seen in the characters of Safo in *Pítaco,* of Zoraida, and the countess in the plays bearing their names as titles. The love need not be that between man and woman, for in *Idomeneo* it is the priest's love for his son that causes him to deny his duty to the king and the nation.

On the whole, the four tragedies comply with the unities of action, time, and place, limiting the action to a single plot occurring in one location and within a span of twenty-four hours. Cienfuegos usually fulfilled these rules without straining credibility, although in composing *Zoraida* he had difficulty in creating a truly unified plot. The blending of the love intrigue with the political conflict leaves the reader with the impression that the dramatist attempted to put too much into the tragedy, as is particularly noticeable in the denouement where, after the suicide of the lovers, an additional scene is provided to satisfy the neoclassical ideal of poetic justice.

The concept of drama as a school for morals is basic to neoclassical theater, whose principal theorist, Ignacio de Luzán, had established the primacy of the teaching function of the dramatist in both moral and political questions. Cienfuegos's plays jointly constitute a theater of the Enlightenment, a theater of propaganda portraying the ideals of the Enlightenment together with the benefits of peace and happiness to be derived from them. Cienfuegos's tragedies, however, also reveal a concern with presenting different points of view. He obviously recognized that tragic seriousness included more than the rhetoric of patriotism and heroism, and so employed the technique of emotional debates between antagonists who propound opposing attitudes toward moral and political questions.

Cienfuegos's tragedies are essentially expressions of eighteenth-century optimism, idealism, and confidence in the goodness of man, with virtue being the most pervasive of his themes. The lesson of virtue was not limited to a personal standard but included a social one, for virtue comprised what is useful for society, morality being meaningless except in the context of human relationships. He promotes the ancient idea that the humble life of the country is superior to the life of power and wealth. The responsibilities and the evils of the courtly life produce only anxiety and grief, while the simple country life fosters virtue, seen as essentially synonymous with happiness in the eighteenth-century lexicon. Other characteristic motifs of Cienfuegos's theater are friendship, patriotism, humanitarianism, justice, public welfare, and reason. A generally optimistic tone derives from the positive lessons of his tragedies, for Cienfuegos advances that idea that reason will prevail and that a utopian state will evolve in which the ruler will use his power only to benefit the nation.

The theater public of the late eighteenth century preferred intensity to subtlety. The audiences wanted to witness or experience intense emotions, and obviously the way to accomplish that end was to portray virtue in distress. Thus a constant trait of Cienfuegos's theater is the depiction of virtuous characters suffering the injustices perpetrated by selfish, irrational individuals who did not listen to the voice of nature. Cienfuegos's use of the death of innocent victims—Linceo and Polimenes in *Idomeneo,* the countess in *The Countess of Castile,* and the lovers Zoraida and Abenamet in *Zoraida*—plus the fall of the virtuous king in *Pítaco,* indicate that the dramatist was striving for strong emotional effects in his plays as well as promoting political and moral lessons, humane attitudes and values. Repetition, broken speeches, and tears create tension and display the conflicts and doubts in passionate human terms. The emotionalism of the tragedies helps to promote the social message as in the sentimental denouement of *The Countess of Castile,* which ends with a demonstration of the humanitarian and political ideals of the playwright.

Las hermanas generosas

There is no proof that *Las hermanas generosas* (The generous sisters), Cienfuegos's only known effort in the comic genre, was ever staged. This one-act sentimental drama belongs in the tradition of the *comedia lacrimosa* (tearful comedy), a genre that Gaspar Melchor de Jovellanos, Spain's greatest representative of the Enlightenment, had experimented with in his *El delincuente honrado* (The honorable culprit).[50] Jovellanos's play, which can only be loosely classified within the comic theater, was written in 1773. This genre broke with the neoclassical traditions, and the opposition to it was based on what the neoclassicists considered to be an unnatural mixture of the two standard genres.

The leading theoretician of the tearful comedy genre was Denis Diderot, a major figure of the French Enlightenment, whose dramatic theories are developed primarily in *Entretiens sur le Fils naturel* (Conversations about the natural son) and *De la Poésie dramatique* (On dramatic poetry). In these writings, Diderot explains the dramatic techniques that he and other French dramatists had already practiced. He did not oppose the aesthetic theories of neoclassicism and was able to accept their dramatic "rules" including the unities, wishing merely to orient the theater toward the problems of society. Therefore, he established his own rules, stating that the new genre was to treat significant subjects in simple, realistic plots. Playwrights should avoid sensationalism and laughter but should appeal to the sentiments of the audience through moving scenes *(tableaux)* emphasizing the physical arrangement of the actors. Cienfuegos may have been influenced by this "rule" of the new genre when he composed *The Countess of Castile*. The tableau created by Almanzor and Sancho kneeling before the dying countess while holding her hands successfully accomplishes what Diderot demanded in his writings on the tearful comedy. Another "rule" for the new genre was the proposal that the dramatist should develop action through gesture and movement in order to increase the realism and, in some cases, the sentimentalism of the play. Here, too, the theory of Diderot may have affected the dramaturgy of Cienfuegos, whose use of pantomime on a silent stage is particularly striking in *Idomeneo,* especially in those three scenes in which the actors remain mute on stage while revealing their emotional or mental states through their movement and gestures. Diderot also desired that these tearful comedies have a strong moral orientation.[51]

The genre that Diderot provided with a name and a comprehensive theory had actually existed previously. The French dramatist, Nivelle de la Chausée, had broken with the comic tradition, producing a serious and sentimental play with a message in the 1730s. As the century progressed, this type of play increased in popularity, perhaps due to the influence of the sensationalist philosophy of John Locke and others, the English sentimental novel, or the demand for more realism, which the tragedies with their elevated personages and grandiloquent language failed to provide, but most likely to the increasing public desire for an edifying theater that appealed directly to the emotions.

The French critic Gustave Lanson provides an excellent definition on the new "serious" comedy, usually called tearful comedy, bourgeois tragedy, or simply drama: "The tearful comedy is an intermediary genre between comedy and tragedy that introduces characters of a private condition, virtuous or very close to being so, in a serious, grave, at times pathetic action that excites us to virtue on our being moved by their misfortunes and on making us applaud their triumph."[52] The usual formula of the genre is not to castigate vice as in the traditional comedy but to show virtue triumphant in a difficult and moving situation.

Cienfuegos's one-act play does not follow Diderot's theory as closely as a full-length play probably would have, but it does have many qualities of the new genre. A notable difference between *The Generous Sisters* and Jovellanos's *The Honorable Culprit,* Spain's finest example of the genre, is the subject. Jovellanos based the action of his drama on the question of legal justice and the duty of a citizen and a magistrate toward a law they consider unjust. The subject of *The Honorable Culprit* was timely, given the considerable debate during the eighteenth century on questions of crimes and punishments, inspired in great part by writings of Cesare de Beccaria. Cienfuegos achieved the desired pathos in *The Generous Sisters* by depicting a perfect example of sisterly generosity and love. While Jovellanos wrote his play in prose, Cienfuegos composed his moral comedy in the traditional *romance* or octosyllabic verse form with assonance in the even verses, a contrast in metrics to his tragedies where he consistently used the hendecasyllabic line.

Cienfuegos dedicated *The Generous Sisters* to his mother, Manuela de Acero. The dedication is significant, for it provides autobiographical information and reveals profound affection and respect for his mother, widowed at the age of twenty-six when he was five years old. Praising his mother for her heroic efforts on his behalf, he virtually deifies her. In his opinion, this one-act play, which he subtitles a *comedia moral* (moral comedy), could find no greater friend than his mother, who is capable not only of equaling but of surpassing the virtue of the heroines. This dedication maintains the sensibility of his other dedications with the repeated use of such words as sensitive, compassionate, fears, tender, anxieties, and friend, and an occasional diminutive form to convey gentleness and affection. The constant expressions of tenderness and friendship in the prefaces to his plays strike the modern reader as trite and conventional, but they must have moved his contemporaries, who would have considered them novel appeals to their sensibility.

The four characters of *The Generous Sisters* are the two sisters, Doña Flora and Doña Irene, their father, Don Prudencio, and the suitor, Don Narciso. The action takes place in a room of Prudencio's home. As the curtain rises, Flora asks her sister what is causing her sadness. In a touching dialogue the sisters reveal their devotion, and Irene speaks of her eternal tears. The tenderness that each sister feels appeals to the sensitivity of the audience with plaintive entreaties repeated for emotional effect.

The cause of Irene's distress is that she is expected to marry Narciso, but she intuits that Flora, who has not revealed her true feelings toward Narciso, loves the young man. Flora effusively describes him as "very kind, very kind" (1.1). Repetition is a characteristic of the style of the play, and together with constant use of exclamations heightens the appeal to the emotions. The sentimental dialogue between the sisters continues with Flora hoping that Irene will marry Narciso and Irene wishing that Flora will marry him because she senses that her sister loves him. The situation is complicated by the fact that their father has told Irene that he wants to marry her to Narciso. There is no relief from the oppressively sentimental atmosphere. In the soliloquy that follows the opening scene Flora declares "My heart is very sensitive" (1.2) (in this play everyone has a sensitive heart). Narciso differs little, if at all, from the two sisters in his sensitivity, and he is equally generous. Narciso fell in love with Flora at first sight and is now upset by her apparent indifference. She pleads that he have compassion for an unhappy woman. As in his tragedies, Cienfuegos establishes a conflict between duty and love. In this case, Flora feels compelled to deny her love for Narciso out of a sense of duty to her sister.

The relationship between the two men is a reprise of that of the sisters. Narciso, whom the generous Prudencio has raised and educated like a son, praises the older man for being "Not a tutor, but a father / And an attentive and tender friend" (1.5). Perhaps the dialogue of this scene best exemplifies the pious exclamations and protestations of virtue of the play as a whole. Prudencio responds with the following modest but pious protestation:

> I desire a good man;
> For virtue, not thrones,
> Is the reward of virtue.
> Son, for my Irene
> I place your virtues
> Ahead of scepters.
>
> (1.6)

An important theme in the literature of the period is the role of young people in selecting a marriage partner, best known via Leandro de Moratín's neoclassical comedy *El sí de las niñas (When a girl says yes)*. Cienfuegos's play avoids the question of the freedom of the young daughter to select her own husband thus eschewing any suggestion of a conflict between generations. Prudencio, a sensitive and generous father, leaves the young people to talk alone. Narciso, thinking that Flora does not love him, informs Irene that he loves Flora, but she will not marry him. Of course, he is unaware that the reason for Flora's rejection is that she wants Irene to have the happiness of being his wife. Irene promises him that Flora will be his wife, even though Narciso vows to keep his promise to marry Irene. The father consents to Irene's argument that the proper marriage would be between Flora and Narciso. Scene 11 finds Prudencio on stage alone in silence, a technique that also occurs in Cienfuegos's tragedies. There are no stage directions, so the actor would have been free to develop the action through gestures and movement, as proposed by Diderot in his "rules" for the tearful comedy genre.

The final scene appeals to the sentiments of the audience through a moving tableau formed when Narciso and Flora take each other's hand and Prudencio embraces his two daughters. Primarily in this scene, but also throughout the play, the spectator is reminded by the constant use of abstractions that moral principles are involved. The strong moral orientation that Diderot suggested for the tearful comedy is obvious in the denouement, as everyone admires the sacrifices made by the generous sisters, each willing to sacrifice her own happiness for the benefit of the other. The final lines are a display of mutual affection and of respect for the virtuous behavior of the sisters. For Narciso, "their example / will be a lesson to me forever" (1.12). The moralizing tendency has been so accentuated in the final scene that the final words of the play almost create the impression that the audience has witnessed a sermon.

The Generous Sisters, despite being a one-act play, has many qualities of the tearful comedy. The tender scenes, the characters who are models of righteousness, the impeccable morality of the action, the conception of comedy as a play to move the audience rather than provoke laughter—all these relate this play to the genre of the tearful comedy. The moralizing tendency is accentuated, and the dialogue immersed in sensibility as the playwright misses no opportunity to draw tears or extol a virtuous feeling. Exclamation marks abound in a dialogue that attempts to move the audience continuously through righteous exclamations and declarations of virtue. The characters are modest, generous, and endlessly eloquent on the subjects of virtue, friendship, duty, and love. All four characters are incarnations of virtue. Without the slightest hint of selfishness, their every word and act is dictated by a desire to help others through the willing sacrifice of one's own happiness.

The public for which this type of play was written wanted to be moved emotionally rather than amused. They desired a sentimental atmosphere that appears to a modern reader as a caricature of real life, with similarities to the melodramas of the past. This play (which Cienfuegos styled a moral comedy) is inseparable from the moral and ideological climate of the time, without which it seems antiquated, almost absurd.

Chapter Five

Minor Works

Speech to the Royal Academy of the Language

Cienfuegos's address to the Royal Academy of the Language, given as part of his initiation, was printed by the Academy without a title. José Simón Díaz, in his bibliography of Cienfuegos's works, calls it "Sólo sobre un Diccionario metódico puede perfeccionarse la Gramática de la Lengua"[1] (Only through a methodical dictionary can the grammar of the language be perfected). This bibliographer appears to have arbitrarily created a title based on what he considered to be the most salient point of the discourse. A more appropriate title might have been "On the Origins and Nature of Language."

Cienfuegos had a great interest in language, considerably beyond that of the average literary figure, as this discourse indicates. Unfortunately, most of his work in the field of linguistics and grammar has been lost. It is known that he did plan two major projects according to a document dated 1785 entitled "Diccionario etimológico de la lengua eastellana" (Etymological dictionary of the Castilian language) and a "Gramática general y filosófica"[2] (General and philosophical grammar). These two possibly uncompleted works must have created some scholarly repute for him among his contemporaries. Leandro Fernández de Moratín, who was often on the opposite side in the literary and political controversies of the time, wrote that the grammar "was a work of a great deal of study and erudition."[3] Antonio Alcalá Galiano, who knew personally many literary figures of the early nineteenth century, declared that Cienfuegos "possessed a great knowledge of the Castilian language."[4]

His speech to the Academy is important because it reveals the poet's conception of language, which in turn illuminates his innovative poetic style. Cienfuegos's philosophy of language permitted him to create new words with impunity and to deviate from standard syntax. The tone of the speech typifies the spirit of the Enlightenment in its optimism and preaching of brotherhood, virtue, and the power of reason. Cienfuegos preaches throughout that the efforts of all men working together as brothers will bring virtue and happiness to society. He states also that literary groups are "formed to carry men through the knowledge of truth to the practice of virtue and to the possession of true happiness."[5] And the result of men working together with each contribution to the knowledge and benefit of others will be "the triumph of human reason" (353). Cienfuegos is adamant in his encouragement of the study of languages because the "word is the vocal picture of thought and, consequently, the art of speaking with clarity and exactness is nothing less than the art of thinking clearly and exactly" (354). He also declares that those periods in history when man was governed by superstition and absurd opinions were epochs in which language was abused and neglected, and he defends philologists from attacks against the shortcomings of grammar, dictionaries, and etymologies by indicating that scholars in other fields have also been mistaken. Deploring specialization, Cienfuegos faults the "learned men who, enclosed in the confines of their favorite field of study, have declared war on those who pay homage to other idols" (356). In his opinion, specialization has created divisions of knowledge, whereas he believes knowledge cannot be compartmentalized.

According to Cienfuegos, the philologists erred in limiting themselves to the study of grammar and the history of language based on the ancient languages when they could have made far greater advances if they had begun their work with a knowledge of all sciences, metaphysical and moral, natural and exact. They would not have considered languages as the arbitrary inventions of men but recognized that all languages are one. In his opinion language is the work of nature, and the variations are products of the different circumstances in which man has found himself. Thus, the philologists "should have looked for the origins of language in nature which would have dictated to them the constant laws that are common to all languages" (357).[6] Cienfuegos, unfortunately, does not explain his concept of nature; however, for his contemporaries at the turn of the century nature was viewed as an omnipotent deity, more powerful than reason, and the essence or origin of all things. This concept can be found in various poems by Cienfuegos, for example, "Spring" and "To a friend who doubted my friendship."

To substantiate his view that all languages are one he states that languages use the same means, that is, oral sounds in different combinations, to express ideas and emotions. If the alphabets of all races are compared, it will be seen that "they consist of the same simple and primitive sounds that only vary in the compound and derivative sounds formed from the simple ones" (357).

Philologists have erred in following a pet theory, seeking the origins of language in a specific source and failing to compare languages in order to extract universal laws, so that "there is no art whose rules are more variable and, consequently, more false" (358) than the contributions of philologists. In Cienfuegos's opinion the supreme law of philology is usage. The true language is not rational and rigid but rather oral, changing according to man's situation in nature. In the literary disagreements over the relative merit of the ancient authors in comparison with the moderns it appears that Cienfuegos would favor the latter. At least he recommends against imitating slavishly the language of ancient masters because language does change, reiterating that the supreme law is the law of nature, which "decides the merit or lack of merit of writers. Those whose expression conforms with their thoughts and feelings speak well because that is the imitation of nature; and *usage* is a meaningless word or it is nothing other than the exercise, the practice of this imitation" (359). It is ridiculous, therefore, to recommend the imitation of good authors; rather, a writer should study the methods that good authors employ in order to imitate nature. The works of good authors are excellent copies of nature and, therefore, the writer who "sets out to imitate them condemns himself to making copies of copies without ever knowing their true prototype" (359).

For Cienfuegos it is inexplicable to declare that all writers should use the words, phrases, and expressions of a few authors from the past who are now considered to be worthy of emulation. Cienfuegos often broke from the established style, creating new words and using unconventional syntax for which he was chastised by conservative critics. In this address, it is obvious that he believed strongly in the freedom of each artist to enrich the nation's language. He states that ancient writers had freely brought new words into the language. The writers of the Renaissance were a weighty precedent because the neoclassicists admired the authors of the sixteenth century: "Read our writers of the sixteenth century, compare them with those of the preceding century, and you will see how many innovations they introduced, how many foreign locutions, how many words, how many phrases, how many Latin, Italian, and French constructions" (360).

He finds two causes for the prohibition of linguistic innovations. First, philologists failed to recognize that languages "are not governed by fixed laws but by erroneous, contradictory and absurd usage" (360). In addition, he blames a puerile, hypocritical nationalism for rejecting foreign words and denigrating the works of other nations while favoring those of one's own. Cienfuegos, a typical eighteenth-century cosmopolitan, viewed this provincialism and xenophobia as contrary to humanity, detrimental to literature, and a cause of animosity among nations. Cienfuegos looked forward to the day when all men would be one and reason would lead mankind to a utopian society, themes of reason and brotherhood exemplary of the spirit of the Enlightenment.

Cienfuegos promotes the publication of a dictionary with a listing of words not in alphabetical order but according to ideas, a concept close to his heart, for he had done considerable work on the subject of synonyms, some of which the Academy had published. This dictionary would also provide information on the formation of words, including root words and suffixes so as to show "the way to form new words in order that the sciences would no longer make use of unintelligible and absurd nomenclatures" (364). Likewise, he encourages the Academy to perfect the *Gramática* (Grammar of the Spanish Language) so as to establish the "inviolate rules upon which the art of language is founded, characterize the different styles, teach the difference between a scientific work and one of pure pleasure, between an oratorical discourse and a historical account, between prosaic language and poetic language" (364–65). In Cienfuegos's opinion an excellent command of the language will necessarily result in better communication and increased knowledge so that "all the sciences, guided by a logical language, will advance rapidly" (365).

Carried away by enthusiasm for his proposals, Cienfuegos foresees the Academy's involvement in the study of language as a major contribution toward the achievement of a utopian world, expressing limitless optimism and faith in the power of reason, in man's capacity for virtue, and in the ideal of universal brotherhood, all of which make this speech a superb example of the spirit of the Enlightenment.

This address to the Royal Academy of the Language makes use of the standard rhetorical devices, including series of exclamations and questions employed for their emotional effect on the audience, and repetition of words and phrases at the beginning of sentences to move the listeners through the rhythm and forcefulness of the words. Perhaps the most striking quality of the address is the sentimentalism characteristic of the literature of the period. Telling the academicians that their accomplishments will make men happy after so many years of ignorance and misery, he states that future generations "will shed tears of gratitude on the tombs of their elders" who sacrificed for the sake of their descendants (366).

Works on Language

Cienfuegos wrote a brief book whose title, *Sinónimos y tratado del artículo* (Synonyms and treatise on the article), is misleading in that the essay does not deal with the article but rather the adjective. The treatise is a thorough discussion of the function and types of adjectives. This work also contains forty-one essays on a total of ninety-one words or expressions indicating the similarities and divergences of their use and meanings.[7] The Royal Press first printed a study of synonyms by Cienfuegos in 1790, with subsequent printings of Cienfuegos's commentaries on the use of synonyms in 1799, 1830, and 1835. The editions of 1830 and 1835 include the work of Jose López de la Huerta on synonyms and the essay on the article.[8]

In his discourse given 20 October 1799 to the Royal Academy, the writer stresses the importance of a comparative study of words, employing the concepts of sign and signified, and appealing to the Academy to undertake the task of creating a dictionary ("Diccionario metódico") "in which the words occupy their place not according to an alphabetical order but according to ideas which is the order of nature. There we will see, with the history of each sign, the history of each thought represented by it and consequently the history of knowledge among us. . . . and determining the difference that there is between so-called synonymous words, you will prove in practice that each sign represents a different idea or a different modification of a single idea" (364).

Cienfuegos firmly believed in the importance of a precise study of the definition and use of words as a means of understanding a nation's intellectual development. It is not surprising that he himself had undertaken the study of synonyms when he encouraged the Academy to provide the nation with a dictionary whose contents would be classified according to ideas. Another study by Cienfuegos dealing with language, a "Gramática filosófica de la lengua castellana" (Philosophical grammar of the language), apparently has been lost. There is no information concerning this work other than the title.

Translations

In addition to his original poetry and plays, Cienfuegos's literary corpus includes translations, speeches, journalistic pieces, and works dealing with language.[9] Cienfuegos translated four odes by Anacreon that, in the opinion of Hermosilla, demonstrate that the translator had a limited knowledge of Greek.[10] Menéndez Pelayo agrees with this critic, faulting Cienfuegos for deviating from the simplicity of the original and employing neologisms.[11] Cienfuegos also translated an ode by Horace that many have judged to be inferior based, according to Menéndez Pelayo, upon the evaluation of a critic named de Burgos.[12] Menéndez Pelayo, however, cites verses from the translation to demonstrate Cienfuegos's skill as a translator.[13]

Cienfuegos also translated the poetry in a novel by the French author Jean-Pierre Claris de Florian,[14] *Gonzalo de Córdoba o la conquista de Granada,* published in Madrid in 1794 and reprinted several times after that date. Cienfuegos's translations of the poems in this novel are, in general, freely done and may be described as adaptations in which the translator expanded the original while maintaining its central ideas. Perhaps one of the more interesting poems adapted from the French is the ballad "Fernando y Elcira" (Ferdinand and Elcira), wherein Cienfuegos paints a typical romantic landscape with arid mountains, sharp precipices, and foamy torrents of water. The wild, primitive nature reflects the torment of the two lovers who, pursued by their enemies, tearfully bewail their fate. The gallant Spaniard and the beautiful daughter of the Moorish king then throw themselves into the abyss, which ever after cries out "Elcira and Ferdinand."

Elogio del Señor D. Joseph Almarza

On 28 September 1799 Cienfuegos addressed the Patriotic Society of Madrid, of which he was a member, eulogizing one of the founders of that society who had also served as its treasurer for many years.[15] Since Cienfuegos admits that he had not had the good fortune to know Joseph Almarza, the fact that he was chosen to deliver the eulogy must be attributed, at least in part, to his reputation as an orator.

The speech manifests the characteristic themes of humanity, brotherhood, virtue, good citizenship, and, in general, the Enlightenment's emphasis on progress and reforms with the goal of a better society for all men.

Cienfuegos perceives contemporary society as a contrast to a past golden age of happiness and virtue, for mankind has lost its innocence and now erects altars to evil and injustice. Only a few "good men" ("hombres de bien") preserve the values of that ideal epoch, the subject of this eulogy having been one of those "beneficent and virtuous" men who consoled the afflicted, aided widows, was a father to orphans, a son to his nation, and a brother to all men (5). Cienfuegos praises Almarza for supporting agriculture, protecting the arts, encouraging industrial development, and overcoming idleness through the education of the young. Employing one of the favorite themes of the Enlightenment, Cienfuegos denigrates the nobility who lead idle, sterile lives, unlike Almarza, who "undertook a career that was most useful to the nation and, consequently, very honorable no matter how much the stupid vanity of illustrious idle men may cause them to look upon it with the greatest disdain" (10). Among other proposals, Cienfuegos urges the Society that "on reforming education, on spreading instruction and industry it should seek the good of all men of all stations and ages with greatest concern for that class of citizens whose poverty reduces them to the greatest ignorance and the most sorrowful abandonment" (37).

His eulogy ends on a theme that occurs elsewhere in his writings, namely, that those men recognized as great are often in reality men who have done greater harm than good, for example, those whose desire for fame and grandeur has resulted in war and suffering. As in his "Ode to Peace" he praises the man of peace, considering true greatness to inhere in love of virtue, peace, and brotherhood.

Elogio del excelentísimo señor marqués de Santa Cruz

Cienfuegos read his eulogy of the Marquis de Santa Cruz, deceased director of the Royal Academy of the Language, to that distinguished body on 11 November 1802.[16] This discourse, like his eulogy of Joseph Almarza, promotes reform and progress in all spheres of Spanish society. Again he characterizes the subject of his eulogy as an ideal representative *(hombre de bien)* of the spirit of the Spanish Enlightenment. The virtuous, philanthropic, humanitarian figure of the marquis recalls the traits of the "hombre de bien" who appears in José Cadalso's *Moroccan Letters*. Cienfuegos describes the "hombre de bien" as one who dedicates himself "to the practice of beneficence . . . a protector, friend and brother of men" (2), stating that "if these men of peace united a fondness for letters to their love of virtue they are even more worthy of living in the memory of posterity" (3).

The sentimentalism of Cienfuegos's other works reappears in this eulogy when he speaks of "tender melancholy" and commands his audience: "Come, gentlemen, come and sprinkle with your tears the remains of an *hombre de bien*" (4). Addressing a learned group, he makes many references to literary and mythological figures of ancient Greece and Rome as well as to moderns like Racine and Newton. At times the elegant, learned style sounds pompous and stilted, as in his lengthy description of the marquis's efforts as a student when "untiringly he persisted until Minerva finally rewarded such painful sacrifices by propitiously opening for him the entrance to her temple" (6).

Not only did the deceased dedicate himself to study, but he wisely spent his wealth on his library, his chemistry laboratory, and his collections of machinery and natural history. In his scholarly pursuits this grandee avoided falling into vices like so many others of his class. The cosmopolitan eighteenth century was an age of travel. Those who could afford to do so traveled extensively, especially to other European countries. The marquis was no exception, visiting France, Italy, England, and Germany, and learning from wise scholars as well as humble craftsman, after which he "returned to his country laden down with a rich booty" (12), having gathered and learned whatever might be useful to his fellow citizens.

The marquis serves as a perfect demonstration that "the love of wisdom, far from being a means of breaking all moral and political bonds, is nothing other than the love of truth and order and, consequently, the basis of all that is good" (13). Being a model of humility without the slightest taint of hypocrisy, this model courtier later was named tutor of royalty, among whom was the future king. The marquis was also a model of generosity, providing assistance to the poor farmers who suffered hardships because of the vagaries of nature. He reformed the lives and customs of his estates and built "on solid foundations the lasting happiness of many families by promoting as the principal source of this happiness the sound education of the children" (22). He was generous to all who required assistance, with his most favored recipients being "the needy artists and friends of the sciences who had been mistreated by fortune" (24).

Cienfuegos also praises this ideal citizen for his contributions to the Royal Academy of the Language, notably the construction of a new building for the Academy and the publication of a magnificent edition of *Don Quixote*. Also under his direction the Academy published an improved one-volume edition of its massive dictionary. This modest, generous, humanitarian, learned, industrious man was an ideal representative of the Enlightenment, a man of truth, letters, love and brotherhood. Cienfuegos portrays the enlightened marquis as a model for others to emulate, to bring glory to Spain through an Academy that will be a model of learning and the envy of other nations.

Chapter Six
Conclusion and Summary

The eighteenth century is an intriguing period because of the enlightened leadership of men like Nicasio Alvarez de Cienfuegos, who believed in the need for reforms in science and the arts, and in an ethics that called for more just and progressive laws. These patriotic reformers refused to submit to the apathy that kept Spain on the margin of European culture. Possibly these Spaniards, though few in number, would have attained their goals if the Napoleonic invasion and subsequent struggle for independence had not brought Fernando VII to the throne, destroying hopes for further reforms in Spanish society. Under the rule of this tyrannical Bourbon, Spain could not continue to innovate and even regressed from what had been accomplished by the reformers.

The eighteenth century was a period in which criticism flourished, an epoch in which Spaniards questioned the values and practices of a society outside the mainstream of European thought for some two hundred years. The literary, scientific, and political figures of the Age of Enlightenment began what is considered the "modern" era in Spain, an epoch that also observed the growth of a new sensibility, causing many historians of the eighteenth century to divide the Enlightenment into separate movements. They have seen it primarily as a period in which rationalism dominated ideology and literature and, therefore, have perceived the rise of sentimentalism as a separate phenomenon that led to the romantic era, a development in literature called preromanticism. This view is too simplistic to explain fully the eighteenth century. The works of Cienfuegos are representative of the complex spirit of the age. Cienfuegos was a man of the Enlightenment in his commitment to redeem the world through the free use of the faculty of reason. Reason in conjunction with a profound sensibility gave meaning to man's actions in the effort to create a better world. In his search for universal happiness, the writer promoted love, humanitarianism, and virtue, which he understood to be the source of an interior or personal harmony as well as harmony among all men. Cienfuegos's poetry and plays are a successful, coherent expression of these beliefs, which form the bases of the epoch's view of man and society.

The categories to which Cienfuegos has usually been assigned have not been wholly justified. To define him as a neoclassic tends to impose stylistic-formal limits upon his literary personality, which is not only inexact, but appears to be a denial of his search for more profound values. Neither does it seem valid to make a romantic of him as did Menéndez Pelayo, who judged him to be one of those "innovators who arrive before their time."[1] Cienfuegos is often far from being a romantic. There is an absence of any rebellious attitude toward nature in his writings: he constantly speaks out in favor of a natural order based on the correct use of reason. Neither do his writings reveal an irrational faith (he appears to have been a Deist like his mentor Meléndez Valdés).[2] Cienfuegos's faith was essentially a natural religion. His prose and verse do not convey traditional Catholic themes; rather his faith coincides with that of the eighteenth-century intellectuals who wished to approach religion from a more rational point of view. Excepting the tragedy *Idomeneo,* his works do not contain blatant attacks on established religious practices. Also, deviating from romanticism were his profound philanthropic spirit and the absence of godlike pretense. Finally, it would be inappropriate to interpret him as a romantic only on the basis of the obvious presence of "sentimental" elements in his writings. European literature of the eighteenth century abounds in sentimental elements originating in the thought of the Enlightenment, which emanates from a basically sensualist epistemology, psychology, and esthetics.

There were fundamental contradictions in the aesthetics of the eighteenth century, that is, between the dogmatic abstract rationalism of a preceptist like Ignacio de Luzán and the sensibility of eighteenth-century empiricists. In the latter view, sensibility was the moving force behind poetic activity. Man, immersed in the natural world, followed its laws and found nature to be the source of sentiments. In Cienfuegos, sentiment at times appears to surpass reason, acquiring rights in opposition to or above reason. Influenced by this aesthetic of sensibility, Cienfuegos decided that the best form of artistic expression was to communicate to his fellowman emotions experienced in nature. In addition, the poet (fulfilling his duty to his fellowmen as an ethical teacher) produced a union of morality and sentiment, perhaps best exemplified by his equation of nature with goodness, beauty, love, virtue, and harmony. In this view, art served in the general reformation of society. Free from established rules and pretensions and the conditions of the established social structure, it could function as an essentially moralistic force in the life and spirit of man. Cienfuegos's literary compositions reflect a primary goal of eighteenth-century literature—to teach and to reform. Of course, the poet's ultimate goal was to achieve the Horatian dictum to delight as well as to teach. Fortunately, many of his verses do attain this happy combination.

At the time when he matured as a thinker and a poet, Cienfuegos found himself in a society that was dangerously withdrawing from the advances attained under Charles III (1759–88). The political direction of those years, coinciding with the youth of Cienfuegos, was toward general reforms benefiting the social and economic structure of the country and favoring freedom in cultural and civil developments. After the French Revolution, however, there developed a fearful, suspicious reaction.[3] An important experience for Cienfuegos was the appearance on the European political stage of the figure of Napoleon. Like so many of his contemporaries, Cienfuegos first saw in him the envoy of a new era of liberty and justice. Later, however, he recognized the decadence and tyranny of the Napoleonic regime.[4] For ethical and patriotic reasons he defied the French General Murat and was deported to France where he died. This faithfulness to a civic ideal confirmed the strength of his convictions concerning right and wrong.

Cienfuegos, a zealous spokesman of the new ideas advocated by the eighteenth-century philosophers, was among the first to introduce a more realistic view of country life. Instead of idealizing the peasants' existence, he depicted the suffering of those who toiled the earth in order to convince his compatriots of the need for reforms. It should be remembered that the agrarian problem was on the minds of many, and one manifestation of this concern was Gaspar Melchor de Jovellanos's well-known and controversial *Informe en el expediente de la ley agraria* (Report on the agrarian law, 1795). His master, Meléndez Valdés, had written in the same vein, but Cienfuegos was more radical in his bitter onslaught against social and economic injustices in the poem "In Praise of a Carpenter Named Alfonso."

In the nineteenth century, the romantic critic Mariano José de Larra called Cienfuegos Spain's first philosophical poet.[5] But it would be an error to consider Cienfuegos solely as an ideologue. On the contrary, he was a passionate sentimentalist, a sensitive writer in the fashion of the eighteenth century who preferred to deal with ideas. This trait distinguishes him and others from the romantic generation whose passion was turned more toward individuals. The egocentrism that occasionally appears in his verses does not detract from, but, in fact, is united with his desire for social reform. Despite moments of pessimism, he never lost the peculiarly eighteenth-century optimistic worldview of the perfectibility of society. He lived and wrote with that goal in mind. The reform program of the Enlightenment constituted a valiant effort to learn about and create a perfect commonwealth. While these men did not succeed, in part because of political circumstances beyond their control, their struggle to attain a spirit of goodwill among men is a legacy that is valid for all times.

Friendship, *beatus ille,* humanitarianism, and other common literary themes of the late eighteenth century appear in the works of Cienfuegos. However, the tone of his compositions is often more intense that than of his contemporaries because he had liberated himself from the clichés of the neoclassical mode. His dissatisfaction with the inadequacy of language endows his work with a modern tone, suggesting the rebellious spirit generally associated with the romantic artist. His occasionally startling use of language and effusive expression of sentiments give a very personal quality to his poems. At times Cienfuegos's compositions suffer from overstatement, an unnecessary repetition of words, and a tendency to create an inappropriately rhetorical or overly dramatic tone through excessive use of interrogations and exclamations. Such infelicities notwithstanding, he merits a prominent position among the poets of the eighteenth century.

Nicasio Alvarez de Cienfuegos died at the age of forty-five. As with many other creative spirits whose careers were shortened, we can only conjecture what he might have accomplished. Nevertheless, it can be asserted with justification that his early death cut short an outstanding career. He undoubtedly would have continued to grow as an artist. He had the temperament to introduce new words and fresh syntactical structures, and likely would have continued to break new artistic grounds if he had lived through the Napoleonic era. Azorín, the perceptive twentieth-century critic, termed him "the discriminating, traditional, and innovative Cienfuegos" who bridged two worlds.[6] Azorín perceived the importance of the artistic innovations by this poet whom he considered a profound, subversive renovator:

Your spirit, your sensibility, your complete organism of an artist, fluctuates, perhaps without your even being aware of it, between a past that is dear to you and a future that fills you with desire. And that hesitant, mysterious, profound, moving fluctuation is what gives your poetry its charm. In your verses, dear Nicasio, I see forms and colors that are beautiful, which I have already seen, but I also glimpse planes, lines, volumes in relief, in groupings, in symmetries, in valuations that I had never seen before.[7]

The foregoing poetic description depicts the aesthetics of Nicasio Alvarez de Cienfuegos, while the poet's friend, Manuel José Quintana, confirms the humanism of this voice of Enlightenment: "From you I learned not to make literature an instrument of oppression and of servitude; never to degrade with either adulation or satire the noble profession of writing; to use and respect poetry as a gift that heaven dispenses to men in order that they may perfect and love one another, and not to destroy and corrupt one another."[8] Together, these statements capture the essence of a poet and patriot whose writings express the ideology and aesthetics of a turbulent period that witnessed the end of one world and the beginning of another. He remains a major figure of this epoch of transition between neoclassicism and romanticism.

Notes and References

Preface

1. R. Merritt Cox, *Juan Meléndez Valdés* (New York: Twayne, 1974), 57.

Chapter One

1. See John D. Bergamini, *The Spanish Bourbons: The History of a Tenacious Dynasty* (New York: G. P. Putnam's Sons, 1974), especially 102–28.

2. Hans Roger Madol, *Godoy*, trans. G. Sans Huelin and M. Sandmann (Madrid: Alianza, 1966), 21.

3. Bergamini, *The Spanish Bourbons*, 121.

4. Raymond Carr, *Spain 1808–1939* (Oxford: Clarendon Press, 1966), 72.

5. Jovellanos had considerable influence on Cienfuegos, who was twenty years younger than the distinguished polygraph and statesman. See Joaquín Arce, "Jovellanos y la sensibilidad prerromántica," *Boletín de la biblioteca de Menéndez Pelayo* 36 (1960): 140 ff., and John H. R. Polt, *Gaspar Melchor de Jovellanos* (New York: Twayne, 1971), 55.

6. For a succinct but informative presentation of the intellectual and political unrest during the period in which Cienfuegos was most active see Carr, *Spain 1808–1939*, 72–78.

7. Ibid., 74.

8. Ibid.

9. Jose Simón Díaz provides considerable genealogical data and documents on Nicasio's family in "Nuevos datos acerca de N. Alvarez de Cienfuegos," *Revista de bibliografía nacional* 5 (1944): 263–84. The information that Simón Díaz found in the archives concerning the family background of Nicasio was used for the poet's admission to the Order of Charles III.

10. *Teatro de Don Nicasio Alvarez de Cienfuegos* (Barcelona, 1836), 235–36; hereafter cited in the text as *T.*

11. Simón Díaz, "Nuevos datos," 272.

12. Emilio Alarcos, "Cienfuegos en Salamanca," *Boletín de la Real Academia Española* 18 (1931):717. Alarcos explains in some detail the actual courses that Cienfuegos took in the field of canon law as well as studies during the other years of his academic life.

13. Alarcos, "Cienfuegos en Salamanca," 729.

14. Alarcos provides a lengthy list of authors with whom Melendez and his friends were probably familiar; see "Cienfuegos en Salamanca," 728.

15. See Jefferson R. Spell, *Rousseau in the Spanish World before 1833* (Austin: University of Texas Press, 1938), 39. Spell cites a Swiss bookseller who observed that the burning of Rousseau's *Emile* created greater interest in the book, causing Spaniards and others to acquire it at any price.

16. Cano reports in *Poesías,* p. 13, n. 8, that the request to publish this edition is preserved in the Archivo Histórico Nacional, "Consejos," leg. 5550, no. 44.

17. José Simón Díaz reproduces an effusive letter of recommendation from Meléndez Valdés to Jovellanos in "Bibliografía de Nicasio Alvarez de Cienfuegos," *Bibliografía Hispánica* 6 (1947): 36–37. Meléndez Valdés warmly recommends his friend and is saddened to see a good man in an extremely needy situation with an old mother and a blind uncle while others "are swimming in abundance through intrigues and deceits."

18. Manuel José Quintana, *Poesías completas,* ed. Albert Dérozier (Madrid: Castalia, 1969), 187.

19. *Historia de los heterodoxos españoles,* ed. Enrique Sánchez Reyes (Madrid: Consejo Superior de Investigaciones Científicas, 1946–48), 5:320.

20. Antonia Alcalá Galiano, *Recuerdos de un anciano;* cited by Cano, *Poesías,* 14.

21. For a view of this group that opposed Cienfuegos, Quintana and their friends, see John Dowling, "Moratin's Circle of Friends: Intellectual Ferment in Spain, 1780–1800," in *Studies in Eighteenth-Century Culture,* ed. Ronald C. Rosbottom, vol. 5 (Madison: University of Wisconsin Press, 1975), 165–83.

22. John Cook, *Neo-Classic Drama in Spain Theory and Practice* (Dallas: Southern Methodist University Press, 1959), 303–4.

23. José Luis Cano has attempted to uncover the identify of this mysterious figure in "¿Quién era Florián Coetanfao?," *Revue de littérature comparée* 33 (1959):400–40; reprinted in *Herdoxos y prerrománticos* (Madrid: Júcar, 1975), 281–302.

24. Cano denies this possibility; see *Heterodoxos y prerrománticos,* 302.

25. For a discussion of the theme of friendship in history and specifically eighteenth-century Spain, see Robert J. McCormick, *The Idea of Happiness in the Poetry of the Eighteenth Century* (Miami: Ediciones Universal, 1980), and José A Maravall "La idea de la felicidad en el programa de la Ilustración," in *Mélanges offerts à Charles Vincent Aubrun* (Paris: Editions Hispaniques, 1975) 1:425–62.

26. Cano, *Poesías,* 21.

27. Juan Pérez de Guzmán, *Bosquejo histórico-documental de la Gaceta de Madrid* (Madrid: Minuesa de los Ríos, 1902), 115. The application is

preserved in the Archivo Histórico Nacional in Madrid, Consejos, leg. 5559, no. 87.

28. Simón Díaz has published Cienfuegos's letter to Godoy in "Nuevos datos," 277–79.

29. Ibid., 274–77; Cienfuegos's application is reproduced on 276, n. 13.

30. *Bosquejillo de la vida y escritos de D. José Mor de Fuentes, delineado por él mismo,* ed. Manuel Alvar (Granada: Universidad de Granada, 1952), 67.

31. Cited by Cano, *Poesías,* 20. Much earlier an unknown critic who used the pen name N. Philoaletheias had cited and praised the poetry of Cienfuegos in his book *Reflexiones sobre la poesía* (Madrid, 1787); cited in José Luis Cano, "Una *Poética* desconocida del XVIII: *Las reflexiones sobre la poesia* de N. Philoaletheias," *Bulletin Hispanique* 63 (1961):62–87, reprinted in *Heterodoxos y prerrománticos* 229–79.

32. José Luis Cano, "Cienfuegos en la Academia," *Cuadernos Hispanoamericanos* 280–82 (1973):611.

33. *Historia de los heterodoxos españoles,* 5:297.

34. This speech is printed in *Memorias de la Academia Española* 1 (1870):352–67. Here the speech is dated 20 October. According to Cano, the minutes of the Academy give the date as 24 October. See "Cienfuegos en la Academia," 612.

35. José Luis Cano, "Cienfuegos durante la invasión francesa," in *Mélanges a la Mémoire de Jean Sarrailh* (Paris: Centre de Recherches de l'Institut d'Etudes Hispaniques, 1966) 1:167.

36. Cited by Cano, *Poesías,* 25; also in Cano, "Cienfuegos durante la invasión francesa," 169–70.

37. For more details on this incident see Fernando de Antón del Olmet, *El cuerpo diplomático español en la Guerra de la Independencia* (Madrid, n.d.), 2:7 174–81. Antón del Olmet calls the refusal to submit to the threats of Murat, that is, the actions of Cienfuegos's colleagues and the Council, an "historical moment in the destiny of Spain" (177).

38. Antón del Olmet declares definitively that "Sick, weak, without any relatives, abandoned by fate, he did not succeed in escaping from Madrid" (*El cuerpo diplomático,* 2:179).

39. This decree is printed in Cano, "Cienfuegos durante la invasíon francesa," 174.

40. Cited by Cano, *Poesías,* 29.

41. Manuel José Quintana, *Tesoro del Parnaso Espanol;* cited by Cano, *Poesías,* 30.

42. When King Ferdinand VII returned to Madrid in 1814 to accept the throne that Napoleon had forced him to renounce in 1808, Cienfuegos's name would have still been among those most honored by the supporters

of the new Spanish king for his defiant opposition to the French. It is not surprising, therefore, that Cienfuegos was honored with an edition of his works published by the royal printing press. This edition, which appeared in 1816, was more complete than the first edition of 1798. One poem that had been included in the earlier edition is missing, an ode to Napoleon honoring the French leader for the homage paid Vergil on one of his Italian campaigns. Cienfuegos himself had suppressed it for obvious reasons.

Chapter Two

1. See César Real de la Riva, "La escuela poética salmantina del siglo XVIII," *Boletín de la Biblioteca de Menéndez Pelayo* 24 (1948):321–64, and Cox, *Juan Meléndez Valdés,* 56–59.
2. For the influence of Fray Luis de León in the eighteenth century, see W. Atkinson, "Luis de León in Eighteenth Century Poetry," *Revue Hispanique* 81 (1933):363–76, and J. Arce Fernández, "La poesía de Fray Luis de León en Jovellanos," *Revista de la Universidad de Oviedo* (Fascículo de la Facultad de Filosofía y Letras), September–December 1974, 41–55.
3. Rinaldo Froldi, "Natura e società nell'opera di Cienfuegos," *Annali della Facoltà di Lettere e Filosofia dell'Università Statale di Milano* 21 (January–April 1958):67–86.
4. Cano, *Poesías,* 179–200.
5. Juan Meléndez Valdés, "Advertencia," in *Poetas líricos del siglo XVIII,* ed. Leopoldo Augusto de Cueto, Biblioteca de Autores Españoles (Madrid: Atlas, 1952), 2:86.
6. Ignacio de Luzán, *La Poética,* ed. Russell P. Sebold (Barcelona: Labor, 1977), 321.
7. See Pedro Salinas's introductory study of his edition of *Juan Meléndez Valdés Poesías* (Madrid: Espasa-Calpe, 1955), and Helmut Hatzfeld, "Gibt es ein literarishes Rokoko in Spanien," *Ibero-Romania* 1 (1969):59–72.
8. Cox, *Juan Meléndez Valdés,* 59.

Chapter Three

1. See José Luis Cano, "La publicación de las 'Poesías' de Cienfuegos: una polémica," in *Homenaje a la memoria de don Antonio Rodríguez-Moñino 1910–1970* (Madrid: Castalia, 1975), 139.
2. Cano, "La publicación" 139–46. Cano provides interesting details concerning the publication of these works. Of particular interest are the varied critical evaluations that appeared in the *Diario de Madrid.*
3. Ibid., 141.
4. Ibid., 141–42.
5. Ibid., 142–43.

6. Ibid., 143–44.

7. Ibid., 145–46.

8. Ibid., 146.

9. See Jovellanos's "Epístola primera" (First epistle) which he addressed to his friends in Salamanca (in *Poesías de Gaspar Melchor de Jovellanos*, ed. J. Caso González [Oviedo: Instituto de Estudios Asturianos, 1961], 117–28).

10. For Meléndez Valdés's use of a similar term, see Russell P. Sebold, "Sobre el nombre español del 'dolor romántico'", *Insula*, no. 264 (1968):1, 4–5, and *El rapto de la mente* (Madrid: Editorial Prensa Española, 1970), 123–37.

11. For a cogent summary of neoclassic theory and sensationalist philosophy, see Cox, *Juan Meléndez Valdés*, 87–100. Concerning the literature of the Age of Enlightenment, he states that there exists "an intermingling of attitudes which have often been considered self-negating, i.e., Neoclassic and romantic" (91). This intermingling occurred because an increased emphasis on sentiment became a integral part of neoclassic literature of the late eighteenth century. See also Russell P. Sebold's valuable study on the origins of romanticism in Spain: "Enlightenment Philosophy and the Emergence of Spanish Romanticism," in *The Ibero-American Enlightenment*, ed. A. Owen Aldridge (Urbana: University of Illinois, 1971), 111–40. On the duality "reason-emotion," see Guillermo Carnero, *La cara oscura del Siglo de las Luces* (Madrid: Cátedra, 1983).

12. Anthony Earl of Shaftesbury, *Characteristics of Men, Manners, Opinions, Times*, ed. John M. Robertson (London: G. Richards, 1900), xxix–xxxi, 216–17. José A. Maravall provides an interesting analysis of the virtue of sensibility and its moral and social implications in *La estimación de la sensibilidad en la cultura de la Ilustración* (Madrid: Instituto de España, 1979).

13. José Luis Cano provides a brief summary of the major contributors to eighteenth-century tearful literature in "Cienfuegos y la amistad," *Clavileño*, no. 34 (1955):38–39.

14. For a study of the "tearful comedy" genre, see Joan Pataky Kosove, *"The 'Comedia Lacrimosa' and Spanish Romantic Drama (1773–1865)"* (London: Tamesis, 1977).

15. Cano, "Cienfuegos y la amistad," 39.

16. These verses recall Goya's famous work entitled *The Sleep of Reason Produces Monsters*. Goya and Cienfuegos were contemporaries who, at least for a time, belonged to the same circle of friends and attended the same literary and artistic gatherings.

17. On the influence of these two writers in Spain, see Spell, *Rousseau in the Spanish World;* Angel del Río, "Algunas notas sobre Rousseau en

España," *Hispania* 19 (1936):105–16; and José Luis Cano, "Gessner en España," *Revue de Littérature Comparée* 35 (1961):40–60, reprinted in *Heterodoxos y prerrománticos*.

18. For a discussion of friendship in the eighteenth century, see chapter 1, n. 25.

19. Carmen Martín Gaite, *Usos amorosos del dieciocho en España* (Madrid: Siglo XXI, 1972), especially chapter 4, which focuses on marriage in eighteenth-century Spain.

20. Martín Gaite, *Usos amorosos,* 130.

21. "Obras poéticas de D. Nicasio Alvarez de Cienfuegos," in *Juicio crítico de los principales poetas españoles de la última era* (Paris: Vicente Salvá, 1840), 2:187 and passim.

22. *Historia de los heterodoxos,* 5:320.

23. Cano, "Cienfuegos y la amistad," 38.

24. José Luis Cano, "Cienfuegos, poeta social," in *Heterodoxos y prerrománticos* (Madrid: Júcar, 1974), 85.

25. Cano cites Juan Valera's statement on the similarities between Cienfuegos's and Rousseau's criticism of the state of society and discontentment with contemporary civilization ("Cienfuegos, poeta social," 86).

26. Ronald M. Macandrew, *Naturalism in Spanish Poetry from the Origins to 1900* (Aberdeen: Milne & Hutchison, 1931), 117.

27. Ibid., 116.

28. According to Enrique Piñeyro "The Desert Rose" is similar to a poem written in 1836 by the Italian author Leopardi: "Cienfuegos," *Bulletin Hispanique* 11 (1909):38–39.

29. According to Hermosilla, Cienfuegos's ode to the carpenter was so celebrated among his contemporaries that, while still in manuscript form, some had learned it by heart ("Obras poéticas de Cienfuegos," 250).

30. Some of Cienfuegos's contemporaries were equally outspoken. Cano provides interesting information on the marchioness de Fuerte-Híjar, a close friend of the poet, whose speech in praise of Queen María Luisa given before the Royal Economic Society on 15 September 1798 was a denunciation of the injustices of Spanish society ("Cienfuegos, poeta social," 97–99).

31. Ibid., 101.

32. *Emile ou de l'éducation,* ed. F. and P. Richard (Paris, 1957), 343, 345; cited by Rinaldo Froldi, *Un poeta iluminista: Meléndez Valdés* (Milan: Istituto Editoriale Cisalpino, 1967), 117, n. 91.

33. See his speech to the Academy of the Language in *Memorias de la Academia Española* (Madrid, 1870), 1:352–67, especially 360–61.

34. *Artículos completos,* ed. Melchor de Almagro San Martín (Madrid: Aguilar, 1944), 749.

35. Gómez Hermosilla, "Obras poéticas de Cienfuegos," 187 and passim.

36. Ibid., 216.

37. Ibid., 194.

38. Ibid., 203.

39. Ibid., 192.

40. Concerning this poem, see J. Arce Fernández, "Jovellanos y la sensibilidad prerromántica," *Boletín de la Biblioteca Menéndez Pelayo* 36 (1960):163–67.

41. Marcelino Menéndez Pelayo cites an article published in 1789 in the Madrid periodical *Memorial literario* that attacks the use of mythology in poetry and favors an empirical approach based on the direct observation of nature: *Historia de las ideas estéticas en España,* ed. Enrique Sánchez Reyes (Madrid: Consejo Superior de Investigaciones Cientifícas, 1962), 3:372–73.

42. Alcála Galiano, *Literatura española del siglo XIX,* 84.

43. On freedom within the neoclassical tradition, see Russell P. Sebold, "Contra los mitos antineoclásicos," *El rapto de la mente* (Madrid: Editorial Prensa Española, 1970), 46–49.

Chapter Four

1. For an account of the life and works of this man, who contributed greatly to the development of neoclassicism in Spain, see Ivy L. Mc-Clelland, *Ignacio de Luzán* (New York: Twayne, 1973).

2. On the influence of Luzán in the eighteenth century, see *Ignacio de Luzán La Poética,* ed. Russell P. Sebold (Barcelona: Labor, 1977), 55–64.

3. Margaret Wilson, *Spanish Drama of the Golden Age* (Oxford: Pergamon, 1969), 48–49.

4. Luzan, *La Poética,* 194.

5. Moratín, *Obras póstumas,* ed. Manuel Silvela (Madrid: Rivadeneyra, 1867), 1:79.

6. René Andioc, *Teatro y sociedad,* 533 and passim.

7. *Diario de Madrid,* 3 November 1790; quoted by Andioc, *Teatro y sociedad,* 519. Chapter 9, "El sentido de las reglas neoclásicas," is a valuable interpretation of the rules.

8. Moratín, *Obras póstumas,* 1:78.

9. Ivy L. McClelland, *Spanish Drama of Pathos 1750–1808* (Liverpool: Liverpool University Press, 1970), 1:218. For a fuller discussion of the genre and the period during which Cienfuegos wrote his tragedies see especially 1:217–67.

10. Ibid., 1:218.

11. The theater of these years developed into a vehicle of education and good taste. For an informative view of the Spanish theater of the final years of the eighteenth century see Jorge Campos, *Teatro y sociedad en España (1780–1820)* (Madrid: Editorial Moneda y Crédito, 1969), especially chap. 1.

12. Ibid., 35.

13. Ibid., 36.

14. Ibid., 187. Chapter 4 considers the era of Máiquez.

15. Ibid., 194.

16. Ada M. Coe, *Catálogo bibliográfico y crítico de las comedias anunciadas en los periódicos de Madrid desde 1661 hasta 1819* (Baltimore: Johns Hopkins Press, 1935), 121.

17. Ronald S. Ridgway, *Voltaire and Sensibility* (Montreal: McGill-Queens University Press, 1973), 185. According to Charles B. Qualia ("Voltaire's Tragic Art in Spain in the Eighteenth Century," *Hispania* 22 [1939]:283–84), a translation of *Mahomet ou le fanatisme* was published in Madrid in 1754. There is also an undated Barcelona edition, probably of the eighteenth century. A translation of this play has also been attributed to Tomás de Iriarte.

18. Simón Díaz, "Nuevos datos acerca de N. Alvarez de Cienfuegos," 277–79.

19. For plot summaries of these plays see Henry C. Lancaster, *French Tragedy in the Time of Louis XV and Voltaire, 1715–1774* (Baltimore: Johns Hopkins Press, 1950), 2:443–47. Mozart made this story into an opera. One major difference is found in the motivation of the priest. In Mozart's opera the priest's motive is purely religious, whereas in Cienfuegos's play Sofronimo uses his religious role to eliminate Prince Polimenes so that his own son may succeed to the throne.

20. Francisco Martínez de la Rosa questions this technique because "a pause that is too long or an improper gesture by a silent actor . . . may seem ridiculous and ruin a beautiful work" ("Apendice sobre la tragedia espanola," in *Obras de D. Francisco Martinez de la Rosa,* ed. Carlos Seco Serrano, Biblioteca de Autores Españoles [Madrid: Atlas, 1962], 166). The use of pantomine on the stage may reveal the influence of Diderot.

21. Jean Sarrailh, *La España ilustrada de la segunda mitad del siglo XVIII,* trans. Antonio Alatorre (Mexico City: Fondo de Cultura Económica, 1957), 612. Sarrailh devotes two chapters to the question of religion in Spain during the Enlightenment (612–707).

22. Ibid., 656. Goya satirizes the adoration of statues and relics in *Caprice,* no. 52, "Lo que puede un sastre" (The power of a tailor) which depicts people kneeling in prayer before a monstrous figure. Goya expressed the following opinion: "It is, however, superstition that makes a whole

people tremble in adoration before a piece of wood that is adorned with the costume of a saint." Jovellanos stated in 1796 "That painters have consecrated their brushes to representing religious marionnettes and the idolatrous people have granted them a superstitious adoration." Both citations are from *Les Caprices de Goya,* ed. Jean Adhémar (Paris: Fernand Hazan, 1951), 93.

23. Sarrailh, *La España ilustrada,* 657–58. The author's conclusions were orthodox in their refutation of both ancient and modern opponents of such worship.

24. Cook, *Neo-Classic Drama in Spain,* 292.

25. Enrique Piñeyro, among others, praised this work highly: "Cienfuegos," *Bulletin Hispanique* 11 (1909):43. Joseph Luis Muñarriz considered Cienfuegos, when *Zoraida* appeared in 1798, to be Spain's most promising tragedian: *Lecciones sobre la retórica y las bellas letras por Hugo Blair* (Madrid, 1798–1801), 4:290. However, the judgment of this translator of Blair's work was colored by his own friendship with Cienfuegos (Muñarriz was a member of the literary group headed by Quintana and Cienfuegos).

26. Cook, *Neo-Classic Drama in Spain,* 293. José Vega classifies the role of Almanzor as one of Máiquez's notable interpretations of the 1803–4 season: *Máiquez el actor y el hombre* (Madrid: Revista de Occidente, 1947), 112.

27. *Teatro de Don Nicasio Alvarez de Cienfuegos* (Barcelona: Antonio Bergnes, 1836), 159–60.

28. Hume, *Modern Spain 1788–1898* (New York: G. P. Putnam, 1900), 84–85.

29. María Soledad Carrasco Urgoiti, *El moro de Granada en la literatura (Del siglo XV al XX)* (Madrid: Revista de Occidente, 1956), 160. Information on this novel as a source for *Zoraida* is taken from this study; see 161–62.

30. *Gonzalo de Córdoba o la conquista de Granada* (Madrid, 1826). Florian's novel was published in 1791, and the first edition of the Spanish translation appeared three years later.

31. The pertinent chapter of this work has the following title: "Chapter thirteen which relates what happened to the young king and his people upon entering Jaen; and the great treason that the Zegríes and Gomeles committed against the Moorish queen and the Abencerraje knights, and their death."

32. Carrasco Urgoiti, *El moro de Granada,* 162.

33. Sarrailh, *La España ilustrada,* 602–11.

34. Quoted by Leopoldo Augusto de Cueto, *Poetas líricos del siglo XVIII,* Biblioteca de Autores Españoles (Madrid: Atlas, 1952), 1:ccii. For comments on various political treatises questioning royal authority and

promulgating the rights of the people, see Nigel Glendinning, "Morality and Politics in the Plays of Cienfuegos," *Modern Language Studies* 14 (1984):69–70, 80–81, 82, n. 7.

35. Lester Crocker, *An Age of Crisis: Man and World in Eighteenth-Century French Thought* (Baltimore: Johns Hopkins Press, 1959), 225.

36. Ibid., 235.

37. Andioc, *Teatro y sociedad*, 393.

38. Cook, *Neo-Classic Drama in Spain*, 294; A. M. Coe, *Catálogo bibliográfico*, 52.

39. Marcelino Menéndez Pelayo, *Antología de poetas líricos castellanos. Tratado de romances viejos* (Madrid: Viuda de Hernando, 1903), 11:249. The ballads referred to are numbers 714–15 in *Romancero general*, ed. Agustín Durán, Biblioteca de Autores Espanoles (Madrid: Rivadeneyra, 1924), 471–73. For the most thorough study of this story in Spanish literature see Ramón Menéndez Pidal, *Historia y epopeya* (Madrid: Librería Hernando, 1934), 1–27.

40. Andioc, *Teatro y sociedad*, 392.

41. Coe, *Catálogo bibliográfico*, 60.

42. Andioc, *Teatro y sociedad*, 393.

43. Martínez de la Rosa, "Apéndice sobre la tragedia española," 168. To substantiate his criticism he cites the two appearances of Almanzor in disguise.

44. *Historia de los heterodoxos españoles*, 5:287. According to N. Glendinning, there is no written proof of this assertion: see "Morality and Politics in the Plays of Cienfuegos," 70.

45. Lester G. Crocker, *Nature and Culture: Ethical Thought in the French Enlightenment* (Baltimore: Johns Hopkins Press, 1963), 265–66.

46. Ibid., 295.

47. Ibid.

48. McClelland declares that "His own sense of lyricism, very Spanish in its warm vitality, in its attractiveness of image, made his love-tragedies readable, if not actable" (*Drama of Pathos*, 1:266).

49. Froldi, "Natura e società nell'opera di Cienfuegos," 61, n. 92.

50. See Polt, *Gaspar Melchor de Jovellanos*, 67–74, for a succinct discussion of this play.

51. Denis Diderot, *Entretiens sur le Fils Naturel*, in *Oeuvres complètes*, ed. J. Assézat (Paris: Garnier Frères, 1875), 6:150.

52. Gustave Lanson, *Nivelle de La Chaussée et la comedie larmoyante* (Paris: Hachette, 1887), 81.

Chapter Five

1. Simón Díaz, "Bibliografía de Nicasio Alvarez de Cienfuegos," 41.

2. Simón Díaz, "Nuevos datos acerca de N. Alvarez de Cienfuegos," 281. According to Simón Díaz, the Royal Press acquired various manuscripts of Cienfuegos, but the promise of publishing his philological studies, except for fragments of his study of synonyms, was never fulfilled.

3. *Obras póstumas,* ed. Manuel Silvela (Madrid: Rivadeneyra, 1868), 3:192. Simón Díaz refers to a study by the Count de la Viñaza that indicates Cienfuegos's influence on a grammatical work of the period: "Nuevos datos," 281, n. 19.

4. *Literatura española del siglo XIX,* 86.

5. "Discurso de don Nicasio Alvarez de Cienfuegos al entrar en la Academia," in *Memorias de la Academia Española* (Madrid, 1870), 1:353; hereafter cited in the text.

6. Fernando Lázaro Carreter, describing Cienfuegos's vision of the role of nature, writes: "Nature, only that enigmatic force, has been the creator of language. . . . The language of nature does not perish with the accumulation of arbitrary acts. The original and natural language exists under the most disparate forms" (*Las ideas lingüísticas en España durante el siglo XVIII* [Madrid: Consejo Superior de Investigaciones Científicas, 1949], 76). Alfonso Cervantes suggests that Cienfuegos is saying that language is an instinctively acquired skill and, therefore, his position may be considered close to that of modern psycholinguistics: "Cienfuegos' Linguistic Ideas," *Romance Notes* 19 (1978):52. This article emphasizes the relationship between Cienfuegos's ideas and modern linguistic theory.

7. On the eighteenth century's interest in synonyms, see Fernando Lázaro Carreter, *Las ideas lingüísticas en España durante el siglo XVIII,* 78–87.

8. For complete information on various editions of Cienfuegos's works, see Simón Díaz, "Bibliografía de Nicasio Alvarez de Cienfuegos," 36–44. Simón Díaz also states that Cienfuegos wrote for Madrid periodicals. These publications were not available to me and, therefore, are not included in this study.

9. Marcelino Menéndez Pelayo provides a bibliography of Cienfuegos's publications and comments briefly on his translations in *Biblioteca de traductores españoles,* ed. Enrique Sánchez Reyes (Santander: Aldus, 1953), 1:340–42.

10. Menéndez Pelayo, *Biblioteca de traductores españoles,* 1:341. These odes appear in Cano, *Poesías,* 83–85.

11. Menéndez Pelayo, *Biblioteca de traductores españoles,* 1:341.

12. Ibid., 1:341–42. This translation appears in Cano, *Poesías,* 97–99.

13. Menéndez Pelayo, *Biblioteca de traductores españoles,* 1:342.

14. Juan López de Peñalver, who was responsible for the Spanish translation of this novel, wrote a dedication to Cienfuegos that clarifies

the latter's role in the translation. Cienfuegos, who encouraged his friend to undertake and publish the translation, also (in the words of Peñalver) "beautified this little work with the verses that are in it." Cano, *Poesías,* 201–17, contains the dedication, poetry, and information concerning this work.

15. *Elogio del Señor D. Joseph Almarza tesorero de la Sociedad Patriótica de Madrid, y uno de sus fundadores* (Madrid: Imprenta Real, 1799); hereafter cited in the text.

16. *Elogio del excelentísimo señor marqués de Santa Cruz, director de la Real Academia Española* (Madrid: Viuda de Ibarra, 1802); hereafter cited in the text.

Chapter Six

1. Menéndez Pelayo, *Historia de las ideas estéticas,* 3:409. José F. Montesinos has questioned the use of the term "preromanticism" to designate the epoch, as if it gave birth to romanticism; see his review of Cadalso's *Noches lúgubres,* ed. E. Helman, in *Nueva Revista de Filología Hispánica* 8 (1954):87–91.

2. Voltaire defined the Deist as "a man firmly persuaded of the existence of a good and powerful Supreme Being who created all beings. . . . he does not embrace any of the sects, all of which contradict one another. His religion is the oldest and the most widespread because the simple adoration of a God has preceded all systems of the world. He has brothers from Peking to Cayenne, and he counts good men as his brothers" (*Dictionnaire philosophique,* ed. R. Naves [Paris: Garnier, 1961], 399).

3. Carlos Corona Baratech, *Revolución y reacción en el reinado de Carlos IV* (Madrid: Rialp, 1957); Richard Herr, *The Eighteenth Century Revolution in Spain* (Princeton: Princeton University Press, 1958); and Julián Marías, *La España posible en tiempo de Carlos III* (Madrid: Sociedad de Estudios y Publicaciones, 1963), deal with the Spanish reaction to the French Revolution.

4. Cienfuegos wrote an ode honoring Napoleon that he later renounced, asking that it not be republished.

5. *Artículos completos,* ed. Melchor de Almagro San Martín (Madrid: Aguilar, 1944), 749.

6. Azorín, *Los clásicos redivivos: los clásicos futuros* (Madrid: Espasa-Calpe, 1958), 101.

7. Ibid., 99–100.

8. Quintana, *Poesías completas,* 335.

Selected Bibliography

PRIMARY SOURCES

1. Collected Editions

Poesías de D. Nicasio Alvarez de Cienfuegos. Madrid: Imprenta Real, 1798; Valencia: Ildefonso Mompié, 1816. Contains poetry and four plays.

Obras poéticas de D. Nicasio Alvarez de Cienfuegos. 2 vols. Madrid: Imprenta Real, 1816 Includes six new poems and the drama *Pítaco.* Omits "Ode to General Bonaparte."

Poesías de Don Nicasio Alvarez de Cienfuegos. Madrid: Sancha, 1821. Reprints the poems contained in edition of 1816. Plays are omitted.

Poesías de Don Nicasio Alvarez de Cienfuegos. Paris, 1821.

Poesías de Don Nicasio Alvarez de Cienfuegos. Barcelona: Viuda e Hijos de D. Antonio Brusi, 1822. Reprint. 1832.

Teatro de don Nicasio Alvarez de Cienfuegos. Barcelona: Imprenta de don Antonio Bergnes, 1836.

"Poesías." In *Poetas líricos del siglo XVIII,* edited by Leopoldo Augusto de Cueto, 1–36. Biblioteca de Autores Españoles, vol. 67. Madrid: Atlas, 1953. The introduction to Cienfuegos's poetry consists of biographical notes by M. J. Quintana and an interesting essay by the nineteenth-century critic Antonio Alcalá Galiano. Volume 61 (clxxiv–clxxv) of this series also contains material on Cienfuegos's life and works.

"Diversiones." Edited by Rinaldo Froldi. *Annali della Facoltà di Lettere e Filosofia dell'Università Statale di Milano* 21, no. 1 (January–April 1968):67–86. Previously unpublished early poetry.

Nicasio Alvarez de Cienfuegos Poesías. Edited by José Luis Cano. Madrid: Editorial Castalia, 1969. Complete edition of the poetry.

2. Plays Published in Separate Editions

La condesa de Castilla. Valencia: Mompié, 1815.

Las hermanas generosas. Valencia: Mompié, 1815.

Idomeneo. Valencia: Mompié, 1815.

La Zorayda. Valencia: Mompié, 1815.

Pítaco. Valencia: Mompié, 1822. Also published in *Teatro español del siglo XVIII,* ed. Jerry L. Johnson (Barcelona: Bruguera, 1972).

3. Other Works

Sinónimos castellanos. Madrid: Imprenta Real, 1790. Reprinted in 1835 along with a study of synonyms by José López de Huerta.

Elogio del Señor D. Joseph Almarza, tesorero de la Sociedad Patriótica de Madrid, y uno de sus fundadores. Madrid: Imprenta Real, 1799.

Elogio del Excm. Sr. Marqués de Santa Cruz, Director de la Real Academia Española. Madrid: Viuda de Ibarra, 1802.

"Discurso al entrar en la Real Academia." In *Memorias de la Real Academia Española* 1 (1970):352–67.

SECONDARY SOURCES

Alarcos, Emilio. "Cienfuegos en Salamanca." *Boletín de la real Academia Española* 18 (1931):712–30. Study of his years at the University of Salamanca.

Andioc, René. *Teatro y sociedad an el Madrid del siglo XVIII*. Valencia: Editorial Castalia, 1976. Important study relating the theater to eighteenth-century society.

Arce, Joaquín. *La poesía del siglo ilustrado*. Madrid: Alhambra, 1981. A major contribution to eighteenth-century studies.

Ayuso Rivera, Juan. *El concepto de la muerte en la poesía romantica española*. Madrid: Fundación Universitaria Española, 1959. Considers Cienfuegos's poetry to have many qualities of romanticism.

Cano, José Luis. "Un centenario olvidado: Cienfuegos." *Revista de Occidente* 21 (December 1964):365–69. Also published in *El escritor y su aventura* (Barcelona: Plaza Janés, 1966). Brings attention to a neglected literary figure.

―――. "Cienfuegos durante la invasión francesa." In *Mélanges à la mémoire de Jean Sarrailh*. Paris: Centre de Recherches de l'Institut d'Études Hispaniques, 1966, 1:167–76. Interesting data on Cienfuegos during a crucial period in Spanish history.

―――. "Cienfuegos en la Academia." *Cuadernos Hispanoamericanos* 280–82 (1973):611–16. Information on Cienfuegos as member of Royal Academy of the Language.

―――. "Cienfuegos, poeta social." *Papeles de Son Armadans* 6 (September 1957):248–70. Also published in *Heterodoxos y prerrománticos* (Madrid: Ediciones Júcar, 1975). A study of social and political ideas in Cienfuegos's poetry.

————. "Cienfuegos y la amistad." *Clavileño*, no. 34 (July–August 1955):35–40. A brief study of friendship and sentimentalism in Cienfuegos's poetry.

————. "Una 'Poética' desconocida del XVIII: Las *Reflexiones sobre la poesía* de N. Philoaletheias (1787)." *Bulletin Hispanique* 63 (1961):62–87. Also in *Heterodoxos y prerrománticos*. Comments on Cienfuegos's curious reaction to praise by unknown critic.

————. "Un prerromántico: Cienfuegos." *Cuadernos Hispanoamericanos*, no. 195 (March 1966):462–74. Also in *Heterodoxos y prerrománticos*. Interesting study of the poet, indicating links to the period of romanticism.

————. "La publicación de las'Poesías'de Cienfuegos Una polémica." In *Homenaje a la memoria de Rodríguez Moñino*. Madrid: Editorial Castalia, 1975, 139–46. A review of favorable and unfavorable evaluations by contemporary critics.

————. "¿Quién era Florián Coetanfao?" *Revue de Littérature Comparée* 33 (1959):400–410. Also in *Heterodoxos y prerrománticos*. An attempt to discover the identity of person to whom Cienfuegos dedicated *Idomeneo*.

Cervantes, Alfonso. "Cienfuegos' Linguistic Ideas." *Romance Notes* 19 (1978):49–54. Interesting study of the speech to the Royal Academy of the Language.

————. "Emotion, Feeling and Language in Cienfuegos' Poetry." *Mester* 6 (1976):24–31. Views Cienfuegos as a romantic poet of nature.

Cook, John A. *Neo-Classic Drama in Spain: Theory and Practice*. Dallas: Southern Methodist University Press, 1959. An important contribution to the history of the Spanish theater.

Froldi, Rinaldo. "Natura e società nell'opera di Cienfuegos." *Annali della Facoltà di Lettere e Filosofia dell'Università Statale di Milano* 21, no. 1 (January–April 1958):43–86. An important study of Cienfuegos's writings. Contains Cienfuegos's previously unpublished early poetry.

Gies, David T. "Cienfuegos: un emblema de luz y oscuridad." *Nueva Revista de Filología Hispánica* 33 (1984): 234–246. Presents Cienfuegos as an advocate of social change.

Glendinning, Nigel. "Morality and Politics in the Plays of Cienfuegos." *Modern Language Review* 14 (1984):69–83. Interesting study of his theater from the perspective of the problems of kingship and the relationship between monarch and his subjects.

Gómez Hermosilla, José. "Obras poéticas de D. Nicasio Alvarez de Cienfuegos según la edición de 1816." *Juicio crítico de los principales poetas españoles de la última era*. Paris: Librería de don Vicente Salvá, 1840, 2:187–256. Negative review of Cienfuegos's poetry by a conservative critic.

Huidobro, Luis Segundo. "Apuntes críticos sobre el distinguido poeta español D. Nicasio Alvarez de Cienfuegos." In *Obras escogidas*. Seville: Real Academia Sevillana de Buenas Letras, 1870, 403–20. Grants Cienfuegos an important place among writers of his time. Treats romantic qualities of his works.

Martínez de la Rosa, Francisco. "Apéndice sobre la tragedia española." In *Obras*. Biblioteca de Autores Españoles. Vols. 148–55. Madrid: Atlas, 1962, 3:164–73. Romantic writer briefly evaluates Cienfuegos's tragedies.

Mas, Amédée. "Cienfuegos' et le Preromantisme européen." In *Mélanges á la mémoire de Jean Sarrailh*. Paris: Centre de Rechereches de l'Institut d'Études Hispaniques, 1966, 2:121–37. Views Cienfuegos as sentimentalist but differing from romantics.

Piñeyro, Enrique. "Cienfuegos." *Bulletin Hispanique* 11 (1909):31–54. General view of Cienfuegos's literary contributions. Judges his plays favorably.

Real de la Riva, César. "La escuela poética salmantina del siglo XVIII." *Boletín de la Biblioteca de Menéndez Pelayo* 24 (1948):3211–64. A valuable study of the Salamancan School.

Simón Díaz, José. "Bibliografía de Nicasio Alvarez de Cienfuegos." *Bibliografía Hispánica* 6 (1947):36–44. Provides data on published and unpublished writings.

————. "Nuevos datos acerca de N. Alvarez de Cienfuegos." *Revista de Bibliografía Nacional* 5 (1944):263–84. Contains important data on the poet's family and life.

Index

Alba, duchess of, 10, 46
Alcalá Galiano, Antonio, 8, 60, 107
Almorza, Joseph, 13, 112–13
Alvarez de Cienfuegos, Nicasio. *See* Cienfuegos, Nicasio Alvarez de
Anacreon, 6, 17, 19, 24, 27, 30, 112
Andioc, René, 87
Aranda, count of, 64
Aristotle, 63, 93, 99
Azorín (José Martínez Ruiz), 119–20

Batteux, Charles, 8
Blair, Hugo, 9
Bonaparte, Joseph, 1, 15, 16
Bonaparte, Napoleon, 1, 12, 13, 15, 76, 118

Caballero, José, 3
Cadalso, José de, 17, 19, 29, 32, 42, 56, 85, 86, 91, 114
Calderón de la Barca, Pedro, 66
Campos, Jorge, 66
Cano, José Luis, 19, 27, 41
Candamo, Gaspar González de, 6
Carlos III, 1, 64, 118
Carlos IV, 1, 13, 76, 89
Carr, Raymond, 3
Carrasco Urgoiti, María Soledad, 77
Cienfuegos, Nicasio Alvarez de

   WORKS—DRAMA
   Countess of Castile, The, 2, 9, 12, 26, 27, 38, 75, 77, 84–92, 101, 102
   Generous Sisters, The, 4, 102–6
   Idomeneo, 12, 67–75, 99, 100, 101, 103, 117
   Pítaco, 2, 12, 92–99, 100, 101
   Zoraida, 2, 10, 12, 26, 75–84, 91, 100, 101

   WORKS—POETRY
   Absence of Cloe, The, 42
   Adonic verses to life in the country, 19, 23
   Angry lovers, The, 33
   Autumn, 30, 39
   Ballad, 22–23
   Beautiful Anadoris, 19
   Bucolic poem on the river Tormes, The, 20, 23
   Desert rose, The, 36, 52–53
   Dirge, 24
   Dirge to the elderly, 20, 25
   Dispute, The, 36
   Graveyard school, The, 9, 38, 43–44, 53, 57
   In praise of a carpenter named Alfonso, 12, 24, 43, 45, 53–55, 59, 67, 118
   Intention, The, 31, 33
   Leave-taking, The, 31, 61
   Lover on the departure of his beloved, A, 10, 31, 32, 59
   Memory of my youth, The, 6, 39, 45, 46
   Monostrophe, 24–25
   My destiny, 28–29
   My solitary spring walk, 39–40, 49–50
   My transformations, 28, 29–30
   Ode to Nice, 31, 37
   Price of a rose, The, 30–31
   Rejected lover, The, 33
   Shepherd's walking stick, The, 42–43, 59
   Song, 23–24
   Sonnet to a mountaineer, 20–21
   Sonnet to a valiant Andalusian, 21
   Sovereign heavens, The, 20
   Spring, 10, 34, 47–49, 56, 108

To a friend who doubted my
friendship, 31, 33, 35–36, 40,
50–51, 108
To amuse her sadness, 19
To Galatea who fled her home to
follow a lover, 36–37
Tomb, The, 30
To my friend on the death of a
brother, 43, 51, 57
To the marquis of Fuerte-Híjar, 43
To the peace between Spain and
France in 1795, 51–52, 113
Violation of the intention, The, 33
Without Cloe, 32

WORKS—PROSE
Eulogy of Joseph Almarza, 112–13
Eulogy of the marquis of Santa Cruz,
113–15
Speech to the Royal Academy of the
Language, 107–11
Synonyms and treatise on the article, 111

WORKS—TRANSLATIONS
Poetry, 112

Clemencín, Diego, 10, 14
Conde, José Antonio, 77
Cook, John, 75
Cowper, William, 49
Coetanfao, Florián, 9
Condillac, Étienne Bonnot de, 6, 34
Corral, Andrés del, 17, 18
Crebillon, Prosper Jolyot de, 68
Crocker, Lester, 83, 96, 97
Cruz, Ramón de la, 45
Cueva, Juan de la, 85

Death, theme, 42–44
Diderot, Denis, 102–3, 106

Estala, Pedro, 82
Euripides, 67, 92

Fenelon, François, 11, 68
Fernández de Rojas, Juan, 6, 17, 18
Fernando VII, 14, 15, 76, 89, 116
Florian, Jean-Pierre Claris de, 77, 112

Forner, Juan Pablo, 18, 82
Friendship, theme, 37–42
Froldi, Rinaldo, 19
Fuerte-Híjar, marchioness of, 9, 12,
37, 38, 44, 46, 75, 84
Fuerte-Híjar, marquis of, 9, 13, 16, 46

García de la Huerta, Vicente, 75, 84,
88
Gessner, Solomon, 41, 48
Godoy, Manuel, 1, 2, 3, 8, 9, 11, 52,
68, 76
Gómez Hermosilla, José, 41, 42, 58,
59, 60, 112
Góngora, Luis de, 58
González, Diego Tadeo, 6, 17, 18
Goya, Francisco de, 3, 10, 46

Hartzenbusch, Juan Eugenio, 79
Herrera, Fernando de, 7, 10
Homer, 6
Horace, 6, 17, 63, 96, 112, 118
Hume, David, 97
Hume, Martin, 76
Hutcheson, Francis, 35

Iglesias de la Casa, José, 6, 18

Jovellanos, Gaspar Melchor de, 2, 3, 4,
7, 10, 12, 26, 28, 35, 45, 102,
103, 118

Kant, Immanuel, 35

Language, poetry, 57–61
Lanson, Gustave, 103
Larra, Mariano José de, 57, 118
Lemierre, Antoine-Marin, 68
León, Fray Luis de, 17, 18
Locke, John, 6, 34, 103
López de Peñalver, Juan, 7, 10, 77
Luzán, Ignacio de, 19, 58, 63, 65,
100, 117

McClelland, Ivy, 66
Máiquez, Isidoro, 66–67, 75
Marchena, José, 3
María Luisa, queen, 1, 76

Martín Gaite, Carmen, 41
Melancholy, theme, 33–34
Meléndez Valdés, Juan, 2, 3, 4, 5, 6, 7, 9, 10, 17, 18, 19, 22, 23, 24, 25, 29, 32, 35, 45, 46, 51, 58, 75, 117, 118
Menéndez Pelayo, Marcelino, 8, 9, 12, 41, 92, 102, 117
Metastasio, Pietro, 31, 37
Montesquieu, Charles-Louis de Secondat, baron of, 6
Montiano, Agustín, 91
Moratín, Leandro Fernández de, 8, 9, 27, 60, 65, 66, 105, 107
Moratín, Nicolás Fernández de, 91
Mor de Fuentes, José, 11
Murat, general, 14, 15, 16, 118

Neoclassicism, 25, 34, 47, 61, 62, 63–67, 85, 91, 93, 96, 97–100, 102, 117, 119, 120
Newton, Isaac, 2

Peñalver, Juan de. *See* López de Peñalver, Juan
Pérez de Hita, Ginés, 77

Quevedo, Francisco de, 27
Quintana, Manuel José, 3, 4, 7, 8, 9, 10, 14, 15, 16, 17, 26, 27, 46, 52, 60, 120

Racine, Jean, 67, 114

Rococo, 24
Romanticism, 33, 34, 39, 42, 44, 79, 84, 91, 116, 117, 119, 120
Rousseau, Jean-Jacques, 6, 7, 39, 41, 45, 48, 55

Saavedra, Francisco, 2, 3
Saint-Lambert, Jean-François de, 6
Santa Cruz, marquis of, 12, 13, 113–15
Sappho, 17
Sarrailh, Jean, 73
Sensibility, theme, 34–37
Sepúlveda, Lorenzo de, 85
Shaftesbury, Anthony, earl of, 35
Shakespeare, William, 64
Simón Diaz, José, 68, 107
Social poetry, theme, 44–57
Sophocles, 92

Thomson, James, 52

Vega, Garcilaso de la, 17, 18
Vega, Lope de, 63, 64, 66
Vergil, 6
Villegas, Esteban Manuel de, 27
Voltaire (François-Marie Arouet), 67, 68

Young, Edward, 7, 42, 44

Zorrilla, José, 85